100 YEARS
OF
GRIFFIN PARK

100 YEARS OF GRIFFIN PARK

DEDICATION: To all those who have queued in the rain to watch their heroes.

First published in Great Britain in 2004 by Brentford FC Limited, Griffin Park, Braemar Road, Brentford, Middlesex, TW8 0NT.

Text copyright © Mark Chapman and Dave Twydell.

Design and layout copyright © Brentford FC Limited.

ISBN 0-9541630-2-8

British Library Cataloguing in Publication Data.

Printed and bound by The Cromwell Press, Trowbridge, Wiltshire.

CONTENTS

Griffin Park floodlight tower, 1975.

INTRODUCTION

Griffin Park is home to thousands of memories stretching right back when the first sod of turf was laid way back in the summer of 1904.

We have tried to tell the story as best we can of this football ground that for all Brentford fans, compares to no other. Illustrative material on Brentford from the pre-second world war days is very limited, as several authors over the years will testify.

Gunnersbury Park Museum, plus the local studies libraries of Ealing Central and Chiswick have again been visited - the latter with the invaluable help of Carolyne Hammond - where we have once again scoured the local reference sections and managed to unearth relevant items.

We present to you "100 Years of Griffin Park."

Dave Twydell and Mark Chapman
September 2004.

Acknowledgements and Sources

There are a number of photographs in this book we have been unable to trace the copyright holder. The owners are cordially invited to contact the Club in writing providing proof of copyright. The authors would like to thank the following in giving their welcome assistance to the publication of this book.

Norman Thomas, Geoff Buckingham, Barry Raymond, Tony Willis, David Harrison, Dave Lane, Martin Bartley, John Hirdle, Graham Haynes, Rob Jex, Phil Roker, Amy Crook, Kelly Harris, Tracey Studds, Peter Gilham, Robin Pearson, Lee Doyle, Stuart Emmerson, Getty Images, Steve Hedges, James Marshall, Carolyne Hammond, Steve Hearne, Tim Street, Yann Tear, Mark Vincent, Jonathan Burchill, Fay Twydell, Matt Dolman and a big thank you to Peter Smith. Please accept our apologies if anyone has been missed out.

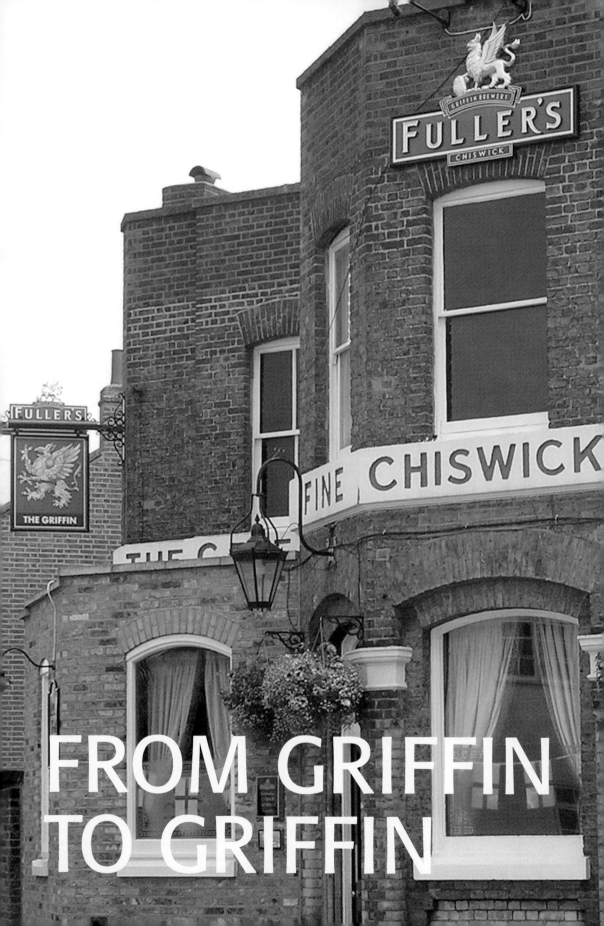

FROM GRIFFIN
TO GRIFFIN

Since the Club's formation at the Oxford and Cambridge Hotel, Kew Bridge, on the 10th of October 1889, Brentford used several venues in the locality before they settled on Griffin Park, literally a stones throw away from their first ground.

The Clifden House Ground (October 1889 - March 1892)

The precise location of this first 'Ground' can be reasonably confirmed. It was described as lying between Windmill Road and Brook Road South, and extracts from various references around this time leave two possible locations: *"...the field at the rear of Clifden House. Mr. Underwood's field." "...at the rear of the Local Board Offices."* "(It has a) *private entrance near to the 'Griffin', the club house, and is fenced in...."* "...elected to defend the Chapel End."* These statements suggest that the Clifden House Ground, as it became known, was the open area between the later Clifden Road and Lateward Road. These references could also possibly refer to the open area that once straddled the line of the later Clifden Road, but all things considered the former of these two locations is more likely the site of the ground. This is reinforced by an inspection of the Ordnance Survey map of 1896 (produced just two years after Brentford vacated the site). It shows an outlined open area measuring around 80 x 55 metres. Short, but conceivably a football pitch size, contained within an outer perimeter - suggesting a proper fenced enclosure. Also two tiny structures can be seen, one at the south-east corner of the field - the location of a refreshment hut possibly, and another at the East end of the 'pitch', a paybox near the entrance. The pitch certainly ran east to west (as at the later Griffin Park), for newspaper references were made to the *"Brook Road"* and the *"Chapel"* ends. The Clifden House Ground, although expected to be only a temporary residence for Brentford F.C., was to become its home ground for well over two years.

The Griffin public house has become synonymous with Brentford Football Club throughout its history. It has featured from the formative days of the Club's history back in 1889 right up to the present. The Landlord of The Griffin was Frederick Allen, a keen supporter of the Club. He offered the use of the pub as a clubroom and as changing rooms. No doubt Allen

Right: A First edition Ordnance Survey map extract circa 1870, showing the rural nature of Brentford. The open space, to the right of the words 'Clifden Ho.' was the site of Brentford's first ground, the space under the word "Rose Cottage" was soon to become the Boston Park Cricket Ground (the Bees fifth home). Griffin Park was to remain an apple orchard for another 30 plus years.

Below: The end of Braemar Road at the junction with Brook Road. Opposite is the opening between the houses to a modern development, but in 1889, this was the entrance to the Clifden House ground. It later formed part of the site of Brentford Girls School.

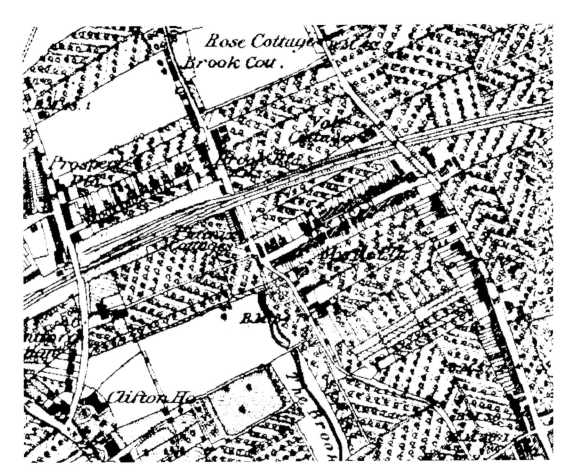

benefited from extra custom, but its location, just a few yards from the entrance to the ground could hardly have been more convenient.

Salmon, claret and light blue were chosen as the Club's colours, the same as the Rowing Club. J.Curtis was elected Club Captain (chosen since he was the only member to have actually played football), and Mr. Underwood was deservedly made the President. In fact salmon was not subsequently used as the Club colours, and for some years the team played in claret and light blue striped shirts with white shorts. Further Club members were sought by way of an advertisement in the local press, and with sufficient numbers having paid their five shillings (25p) annual membership fee, the Club organised its first practise match on the 26th of October. Several other such games were staged before the big day - Saturday the 23rd November - when Kew F.C. were entertained at Clifden House, for the first ever game played by Brentford F.C.

On a damp afternoon, the match kicked off at 3.30 pm, somewhat after the planned time, due to the late arrival of the opposition. There were few present to herald the arrival of the new club, for the gate money amounted to just 2/6d. (12.5p), which would have represented perhaps twenty or so spectators. The honour of the first ever goal, scored early on, by Brentford F.C. fell to Bonnell. The match ended all square at 1-1.

The last first team match played at the Clifden House ground was on the 12th of March 1892, when Brentford entertained The Loyola (Westminster) - for which no result has been traced. The open site of the Clifden Road Ground remained until around the First World War, when the Brentford Girls Secondary Modern School was built, and which overlaid the west end of this, Brentford's first home venue. The rest of the site remained fairly open for many years, and the entrance, located opposite the Griffin Pub at the corner of Braemar and Brook Roads, was still present until the late 1990s, and is still visible as the entrance to a new housing development.

In addition to the Clifden House Ground, an alternative home venue was also used, at least for the pre-season Practise Match on the 20th of September 1890 and for some reserve matches in the 1891/92 season. The location was Montgomery's Field in Windmill Road, previously occupied by, and known as, George Clark's. He lived at Boston Lodge, which was located alongside The Ride. The Lodge ran between Boston Road and just south of the current Windmill Road and Swyncombe Avenue junction. The Lodge in turn was at the north end of a large six-acre field, and therefore logic dictates that this was the aforementioned 'George Clark's Field'. Although no doubt unenclosed at this time, it was used for reserve matches only. A few years later this field became

Right: The Plough Public House around 1900. This rebuilt pub still lies on Northfields Avenue, near the junction of Little Ealing Lane. This establishment was used as the clubroom and provided changing rooms for the club when they played at Benn's Field. To the left of the photograph there was an entrance (which still exists today) that led via a footpath to the playing field. In the distance (between the building and the tree) was the entrance to Ealing Park where Brentford played just one match, in September 1894.

Left: Northfields Lane (now Avenue) near "The Plough", looking north in 1903. The Benn's Field ground (out of sight) was two to three hundred yards to the right.

known as Shotter's Field, and was later destined to become the third home ground of Brentford F.C.

On the 18th of February 1892 the Club held its first dinner at The Castle Assembly Rooms. Aware of the difficulty of finding a suitable ground for the fledgling football club, the view was first expressed at this gathering that the local Boston Park Cricket Club, who had their ground conveniently situated between Ealing Road and Brook Road North, should consider an amalgamation with Brentford F.C. In fact many football clubs around this time were winter offshoots of an established cricket club, and although the two organisations in Brentford were destined to have a relationship a few years later, they never actually amalgamated. In fact, their relationship was for the most part, a somewhat uneasy one.

Brentford's move from their first home venue was probably brought about by two reasons. Firstly, Mr. Underwood passed on the ownership of the land around this time, and for whatever reason, the new owner may not have wished to lease the site to the football club. In addition, the Club, conveniently located in the town, had become popular with the locals and consequently they were well supported. Whilst this was good for the Club, it also no doubt annoyed the local residents since inevitably matches also attracted the unruly element within the population. Brentford F.C. were now faced with a big problem, for they had no ground to play on for the coming season. Whilst at this time the surroundings of Brentford were largely undeveloped and contained many fields, few were suitable for enclosure, and the owners of those that were showed reluctance in letting them out to a football club. The Club was in a desperate state as the weeks dragged on and no suitable venue presented itself. Eventually a field was offered, but it was hardly ideal. However, with the football season having already started, the Club had little choice but to accept it.

Benn's Field, Little Ealing (October 1892 - December 1894).

Benn's Field, as it was known, was located in Little Ealing, well over a mile from Brentford, which at least may have eliminated the 'unruly element', but it was also feared that this somewhat distant location would have a detrimental effect on the support of the much needed respectable spectator. This fear it later transpired was well founded. Although the B's' stay was limited to a little over two years, in some respects this home ground became perhaps the most charismatic of their 'temporary' homes. The Club had previously used The Griffin as a clubhouse and for changing rooms but with it now being located so far away this was no longer possible. Once again, the Club looked to a public house to serve such a purpose, and once again one such establishment was ideally situated nearby.

Above: Inside The Plough circa 1900. With a little imagination one can see the players sitting around the benches in this low-roofed bar drinking their ale after a match on nearby Benn's Field.

The Plough became a local celebrity for it supposedly once entertained the highway robber Dick Turpin - some credence was added to this assertion when a pistol was discovered hidden away on the premises when they were rebuilt in 1906. It was a focal point, located, as it still is, at the merging of Northfields Avenue and Little Ealing Lane, and opposite the junction with Windmill Road. The Plough was the only pub in the area, which at this time was completely surrounded by fields and with very few other structures around. Adjacent to The Plough was an ornate arch over the entrance to the "Bowling Greens and Pleasure Grounds".

Benn's Field extended from Little Ealing Lane north to the railway line (now the Heathrow branch of the Piccadilly tube line) and a couple of hundred yards from the pub and Northfields Avenue. Earlier, the eleven plus acre field had been known as Stone's Meadow and by 1851, a market gardener Charles Benn had bought it. When The B's moved to Benn's Field, Charles Benn was also running The Plough.

A footpath ran across The Pleasure Grounds, which presumably was the near three acre field adjacent to the pub, alongside Northfields Avenue and on across Benn's Field, thereby a one to two hundred yard stroll from dressing rooms to the football field. The large field was big enough for two football pitches, and on occasions both first and reserve teams were known to play there at the same time. But enclosing the venue must have been a nightmare, set as it was in an open field. It is doubtful if the whole area was fenced, but possibly was limited to just the main pitch area, which it is believed lay alongside or close to the railway. The railway embankment would have provided a degree of screening, although the footpath across the field continued over the railway bridge at the end of the ground, and gave a free view of the football action, the *"cheap gallery"* as the *County of Middlesex Independent* once described it.

Benn's Field was never regarded as a permanent home in view of the long trek to watch matches from Brentford. The Club's officials could only speculate on the degree of support that the team could command. Rather than the average of around 400, they should have a better location for their headquarters.

Having played all their early season matches "away" did not

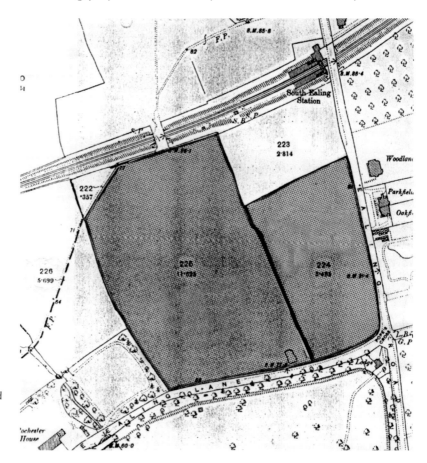

Right: Benn's Field (left) with The Plough pub in the bottom left corner, and the smaller Cross Roads Ground on the right, to the bottom right is Pope's Cross.

prevent the team from making an excellent start to the season, with five straight victories, and this continued with the first at Benn's Field, an Alliance League match versus Kensal, that was played in sunny weather. One week earlier, a 'home' match had been played against Clarence (a 2-1 victory) in the Middlesex Junior Cup. The game probably took place on Mr. King's Field in Boston Road where the reserves also played. This field could well have been that which lay alongside and to the west of George Clark's - later Shotter's - Field.

The increased interest in the club led to the suggestion that 'match tickets' should be issued that covered all home games, and with the cost agreed at two shillings and sixpence (12.5p), the first season tickets were issued by Brentford F.C. But despite a general upbeat air about the Club, there was still concern regarding the ground, not only with regard to its location but the rent that had to be found and running expenses. Accordingly, Club membership was raised by 50% from five shillings to seven shillings and sixpence (38p)

During the Summer of 1894, at the Club's AGM, one of the three other local sides that had sprung up, St.Paul's, amalgamated with Brentford, which ensured a good quality reserve team for the coming season. Another major change was the appointment a new Club Chairman, Bill Stephenson, and he was instrumental in at last finding a new and more suitable home for the Club. This had always been at the top of the agenda, and the chosen venue fulfilled the requirement of it being closer to Brentford itself. Just before Christmas 1894, Shotter's Field was secured.

Before the move, a single match was played on a different 'Ground' at Ealing Park, which in fact had been the home ground of the former St. Paul's Club. This venue was located close to The Plough, but on the other side of Little Ealing Lane. Parsons Green were entertained in a friendly, and scored six goals to the homesters four on the 15th of September 1894. But this experiment was never repeated for it was found that the playing pitch was not wide enough.

The last match at Benn's Field was on the 15th of December 1894,

Below: A match poster on a wall at Brentford Half Acre advertising the forthcoming match at Shotter's Field with the 2nd Grenadier Guards on the 29th February, 1896. The result of this fixture has never been traced. As was common practise, admission for ladies was free.

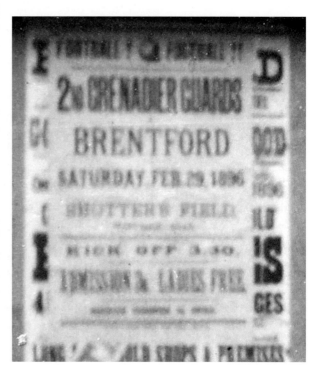

when Darfield were beaten 5-0 in the Middlesex Senior Cup.

S h o t t e r ' s   Field (December 1894 - April 1898)

Lt.Col Stracey Clitherow now owned Shotter's Field plus much of the surrounding area. He also resided in the adjacent Boston Lodge. Presumably the land and lodge had been bought from Mr. Clark, and the Colonel now leased the field to Mr. Shotter and Mr.Veysey. 'Shotter's Field' as it was now known was sub-let to Brentford F.C.

Although far from ideal, Shotter's Field was destined to become the home ground of The B's for nearly four years. It was described in the local press as: *"One of the best in Middlesex. It is dry, very level, and quite close to the town."* At this time there were no facilities at Shotter's Field, and at the start of the 1894/95 season it was not enclosed. It was certainly closer to the town, being little more than half the distance than that to Benn's Field.

Above: A club membership card for the 1897/98 season. Note the ground at this time - Shotter's Field - is also referred to as 'Windmill Road', and the headquarters as the Duke of York Pub in York Road, adjacent to the Boston Park Cricket ground.

Whilst the playing surface and the location may have been right, the ground was initially completely lacking in facilities and enclosure. No record of changing rooms has been recorded, but perhaps a temporary tent type structure may have been used, these being quite popular around this time. Preventing free viewing of matches must have been all but impossible, for Windmill Road ran immediately adjacent, on the east side, and hoardings obliterating the view were not erected until April 1896, and even then in order to avoid paying, adjacent trees were often climbed for a free view. The Ride, which ran between Boston Manor and Windmill Roads, may have been already fenced or tree lined, which would have given some privacy. In the north-west corner of the ground was a small pond, where it was reported on occasions that the ball was lost... *"At one point in the match, the ball was lost in the pond after flying over the spectators."*

Despite the apparent shortcomings of Shotter's Field, the Club was honoured when in March 1895; the venue was used for a representative match between the Middlesex F.A. and the Surrey F.A. During the summer of 1895, a reserved enclosure was incorporated at Shotter's Field. However, it is unlikely that this

Left: The formerly named "Duke of York" Pub, is still located on Brook Road North, and now faces onto the main Great West Road, immediately behind the site of the Boston Park Cricket Ground. This pub was the club's headquarters whilst the team was based in Windmill Road (Shotter's Field) and at the Cricket Ground.

area provided any cover for spectators.

At this time the ownership of the land changed again, and now it was a Mr. Beldam who became not only the new owner of the ground but who also occupied Boston Lodge. Mr. Beldam was no football lover. Although he allowed the continued use of the field for the 1896/97 season, it became apparent that this was with some reluctance. Another factor that didn't help the Brentford cause was the fact that such sub-letting, which continued, was frowned upon, and having in effect two landlords made the rent to the football club very high. But with no suitable alternative the Club had little choice but to grin and bear it. As the season wore on Mr. Beldam became more antagonistic, and in particular he complained about the noise from the crowd that could be heard from the Lodge.

Despite Brentford offering a higher rent, Mr. Beldam steadfastly refused the continued use of the field, a decision that put the Club in a desperate state. However, an agreement was eventually reached between the two parties - probably by way of an even higher cash inducement - and so Shotter's Field continued to be used for the 1897/98 season. By now support for the B's was ever increasing (therefore at least they could probably afford the extra expense), and crowds of around a thousand were not unheard of. The Club entered the F.A.Cup for the first time this season, and after easily disposing of the Coldstream Guards by 6-1 in the 1st qualifying round, in the next tie versus the 3rd Grenadier Guards, a new record attendance of 2,000 was present (a 1-1 draw); the entrance charge was increased to 6d. (2.5p) for this match.

An interesting fixture in February saw Brentford entertain famous Scottish First Division side St. Bernards from Edinburgh.

This illustrates the fact that the Club, now regarded as one of the top outfits in London, had risen to a high status by being able to compete against such opponents, albeit they lost the game 3-0, before a crowd of 2,000.

Now playing in the London League the team enjoyed an exciting season, and when they played Thames Ironworks (later West Ham United) at Shotter's Field on the 23rd of April, the encounter was a top of the table clash. A new record crowd numbering 3,500 (including an estimated 500 visiting supporters) turned up to see the local favourites edge past the visitors courtesy of a Lloyd goal. But this was still not enough for the Championship, which later went to the Ironworks, by just one point more than the B's.

With the Club's fortunes at a high both on the field and at the turnstiles. Attendances were very good and for the third season running had increased. Mr. Beldam realised that this was not an opportunity to miss and for the 1898/99 season he demanded even more rent. This time the committee of the football club refused to be blackmailed, and declined the invitation, telling their landlord that the use of Shotter's Field wouldn't be required for the coming season.

Boston Park Cricket Club had played for some years at a ground on the west side of Ealing Road, just north of the railway lines (adjacent to the later Great West Road), and for the previous two years there had been plans to turn this into a sports ground which would be an ideal solution for Brentford F.C. However, it would appear that this assumption was somewhat premature, for no sports ground was built, and so The B's were left in limbo again during the Summer of 1898, with a successful team but with nowhere to play.

The situation now was desperate, for there was no chance of re-negotiating with Mr. Beldam (there had been talk of development of the site but this did not materialise for many years) and his Shotter's Field, and Benn's Field, were now also out of the question since building on the latter site was soon expected. Any suitable sites near Brentford itself were not possible, and so, reluctantly, the Club had to look for a new home once again. Eventually a field was found, not ideal, but at least somewhere which would serve their purpose for a while.

The last match at Shotter's Field was on the 30th of April 1898, when Barking Woodville were entertained, when the game ended scorelesss in the last London League match of the season, before a *"good attendance"*. Despite such a successful season on the field, the Club had suffered a financial loss over the period.

The Cross Roads Ground (3rd September 1898 - 28th April

1900)

In the past the name of this ground has been given as the "Cross Road Ground", suggesting that it was located in Cross Road. However, there is no road of this name in the area, and in fact it refers to the cross roads, i.e. the intersection, of Ealing Road and Little Ealing Lane, where at this time there was a marker post, literally known as 'Pope's Cross' - which was no doubt related to nearby Pope's Lane. This field was on the north-east corner of the intersection and immediately abutted part of the former Benn's Field. This 5.5-acre field was perfectly suitable in size, but was bereft of any facilities, and once again located a good distance - about a 15-minute walk – from Brentford itself. The Club were able to use the venue by virtue of the fact that its occupants, Brentford Celtic F.C., agreed to an amalgamation with The B's. Although far from perfect, it did offer a home venue for matches, and could be accessed by horse-drawn buses from Ealing and Kew Bridge, plus the nearby District line trains that stopped at South Ealing station.

Above: The top end of Windmill Road, looking South towards Brentford circa 1900. The building on the far left was situated at the junction with 'The Ride' and behind this (but not visible in the photograph) was the Shotter's Field Ground between late 1894 and 1898.

It was reported on the 13th of August that *"Cutting and levelling of the ground are in progress at the present"*, thus suggesting that initially this was nothing but an uneven and rough grass field. Two weeks later, at one end of the ground, a corrugated iron makeshift structure was hastily erected - a pavilion as it was called was possibly an overstatement - to use as dressing rooms, plus a refreshment bar. But there was little, if anything, else, and with the uneven pitch having a pronounced slope, and being somewhat narrow, it was hardly an auspicious venue for this successful team.

Overall the team had, at best, only a moderate season, for

their successes of the past had led to some of the best players departing for bigger clubs, and in order to induce replacement amateurs the Club began paying expenses higher than considered normal. One such transfer was Charles Field who went to Sheffield United. As part of the deal the Yorkshire team played in a Cross Roads friendly match, just two days after they won the F.A.Cup at the Crystal Palace. Seven of the cup-winning team were amongst the eleven who thrashed a lack-lustre B's by 5-2. The only good point was the crowd of around 4,000, which became the record attendance at the Cross Roads ground.

Problems mounted for the Club, for the crowds were down in numbers for normal matches, and consequently the gate receipts slumped - down by around £100 - and the Club were £180 in the red. At the Club's AGM during the summer of 1899, there was disquiet expressed over the presentation of the accounts, and some of the items therein, especially the £318 spent on players' "travelling expenses". It was becoming obvious that rather than a purely amateur Club, Brentford were employing underhand professionals despite their registration as an amateur organisation. The question of forming the Club into a Limited Company was not passed, the books were not audited properly, and whilst these problems and all the other wrangling proceeded, registration to the Middlesex F.A. and London F.A. was overlooked. Consequently this excluded the Club from entering several, often financially worthwhile, cup competitions. With total gate takings down to about a third of that at Shotter's Field, an attempt was made to return there in August 1899, but it was all to no avail.

And the situation got even worse the following season, not only on the field, where the spectators were just not prepared to travel the extra distance. Even lowering the entrance charge to 4d (less than 2p) had no effect. But potentially even more damaging was the question of the Club's amateur status. In late October, the Middlesex F.A. set up an enquiry to look into the Club's affairs. It transpired that books and documents pertaining to the running of the club had been destroyed, and illegal payments had been paid to "amateur" players. It was admitted in the football press that Brentford's case was not an isolated incident of 'shamateurism'. It was generally felt that the club was dealt with harshly when they were suspended from playing for a month, and several of the Club's officials were banned. During the suspension period a new committee was formed, notably under the leadership of Mr. Edwin Underwood, and the club formerly turned professional.

The public appeared to rally round the club; and the first match after the layoff saw the B's play a "Kaffirs XI" from South Africa before a 2,000 crowd. But this was a one-off match, and for the rest of the season the attendances were poor. When Upton Park visited Cross Roads, the gate amounted to just £3, a "crowd" of under 200. A meeting was called at the end of January 1900 when the question of the club continuing was discussed. Despite many members not having paid their annual subscriptions, a good sum was raised at the meeting, at least enough to see through the rest of the season.

Mr. Underwood, the owner of Brentford's first ground at Clifden House, was able to realise an ambition he and a number of other members had when he managed to persuade the Committee of the Boston Park Cricket Club to groundshare with the footballers. In the early days he expressed the wish that the two clubs should form closer links, and although there was no question of a merger, the pair would certainly be physically closer. It was an ideal arrangement, for the agreed rental at the Cricket Ground of £40 per annum would pay off the cricketers debts, and more importantly for the football club, they would at last be based back in Brentford. To cap it all, the local tradesmen who were owed a total of £100 agreed to write off the debt. A dreadful season had at last ended, which saw the team finish third from bottom in the Southern league Division 2, and one that saw the club come close to folding. Now, with a new ground, it was hoped that the dawn of the new century would also bring about the dawn of a new beginning for the B's.

The last game at Cross Roads was on the 28th of April when Southall were entertained and beaten 6-0 in a Southern League Division 2 match before an attendance of 800. Perhaps rather than the result, the biggest celebration was that the club's two-year stay at the Cross Roads had come to an end.

Mr Underwood was deservedly elected President and the club were able to make this fresh start in their first full season as a professional club and at a far more suitable playing venue. However, even at the Boston Park Cricket Ground there was still much to be desired. The ground was located to the west side of Ealing Road, with the Duke of York pub - which had earlier become the club's headquarters. It backed on and was adjacent to the route of the much later Great West Road; just a couple of long goal kicks from an orchard that in four years was to become Griffin Park. This venue was the Sports Ground that had been spoken of in the previous few years, but not located near Boston Park itself, which it is often erroneously assumed.

The Cricket Club had been around longer than the footballers, and had the ground as their venue at the time of the formation of Brentford F.C. eleven years earlier. The enclosure was certainly big enough and was fenced, but facilities for spectators were,

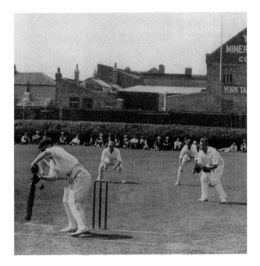

Above: The only known photograph of the Boston Park Cricket ground - looking from the East towards York Road (the Duke of York, out of the picture, would be to the right). This was taken in August 1932, nearly 30 years after the club vacated the ground, and was soon to be developed for industrial use. This shot was taken when Brentford met Arsenal in a charity cricket match.

again, very limited, with no cover and barely any seating. There were two small pavilions, no doubt used as changing rooms and for the use of a very limited number of members. These structures were located on the north side of the ground, one in the corner adjacent to Ealing Road, and the other located midway down the side. The club immediately set about persuading the cricketers of the benefits of erecting covered enclosures, which initially they were vehemently opposed to. But eventually the football club won them over, and during this the first season at the ground; they set about raising funds for this big project.

The Boston Park Cricket Ground, York Road. (15th September 1900 - 2nd April 1904)

The first match played at York Road was versus Chesham Generals in a friendly before a large crowd of around 3,000. The local MP was present when the ground was formally opened, assisted by the Club Chairman and Secretary, whilst the Isleworth Town Band started the proceedings.

After an astonishing 12-1 London League victory at Barnet, the team slumped to two York Road defeats, before the first Southern League match at the new venue. By coincidence, a visit was made by Southall F.C. (the last opponents at the Cross Roads ground), a fixture that finished goalless before another excellent crowd of 3,000. The B's were lucky to pick up a point, surviving several narrow escapes, and the visitors had two goals disallowed. Running a joint first team in the two leagues, the players came good in the major competition and at the end of the season were crowned as Champions. Only two points were dropped (in drawn matches) and impressive victories included a 9-1 thrashing at Southall and 11-1 at home to Wycombe Wanderers. Unfortunately, there were only around a thousand present at York Road to witness this feat. Automatic promotion had not been introduced at this time, and reminiscent of happenings nearly a century later, Brentford were unable to win the play-off match.

Club officials were determined to attain Southern League First Division status. They reasoned that already support was increasing, and with new tram routes leading to Brentford, this would open up a greater catchment area. At the Club's A.G.M. they announced the intention to form a Limited Company with a capital of £1,000, which would allow ground improvements at

York Road. But a final decision would not be made until after the Southern League's annual meeting on June the 1st. The first course of action was to apply for the position vacated by the Bristol City's election to the Football League, but the club was dismayed when Northampton Town, with only a moderately successful Midland League playing record, were elected at the B's expense.

Later in June the re-convened A.G.M. vowed to proceed with their ambitious plans regardless, although one month later their wish was granted when the B's were elected to the First Division, following the late withdrawal of Gravesend United. This elevation was on the strict understanding that Brentford would strengthen their team, which they duly did. The Brentford Football and Sports Club Limited emerged on the 27th August 1901, with a share capital of £2,000, but this was not the end of the close season dramas. The Cricket Club decided they had had enough of the footballers "damaging the pitch" and announced they would not be leasing it out for a second season. This brought about the condemnation of the cricketers with the allegation that they only allowed the footballers the use of the ground for one season in order to clear their own debts. Eventually an agreement was reached, and for the sum of £40, the B's had a home for the 1901/02 season.

The new lease started on September the 1st, and the football club had just a few weeks to install temporary covered stands - the "flower pot" stands as they became to be known (at the Ealing Road end) plus earth banked terracing (at the York Road end) and hot showers and baths in the pavilion, all required by the Southern League rules; amazingly these changes were allowed by the Cricket Club to be carried out without objection. Included on the first Board of Directors were Bill Dodge and Harry Blundell who were both involved with the club from its inception, each holding their directors positions for no less than fifty years.

The 1902/03 season, the team's second in the Southern League First Division, started in much the same way as a year earlier. A dreadful campaign was only relieved by the fact that attendances - at least for the principal Southern League matches - actually increased despite the lack of success on the pitch, plus an exciting run in the F.A. Cup. Oxford City were beaten in the 3rd qualifying round after a replay, followed by a local derby home victory over Southall before a 2,400 crowd. Three games were required to

Below: A Brentford team group from 1900-01, who won the Second Division of the Southern League in their first season at York Road.

overcome another local side, Shepherds Bush, before the final qualifying (intermediate) round when Woolwich Arsenal were entertained at York Road.

This cup match attracted unprecedented interest and special arrangements had to be made to accommodate the record crowd. In an incredibly short space of time the necessary additions were made. The flower-pot stands were doubled in size, the York Road end was banked and extra entrances and exits were installed at both ends of the Ground. Yet despite all the preparations, on a cold and wet December the 13th, the crowd only numbered around 7,000, with receipts of £172, although easily a new record for Brentford at the York Road enclosure. A creditable 1-1 draw was played out, after no goals up to half-time, but in the replay at Plumstead, despite holding out in the first half, the B's finally succumbed by 5-0.

Another good cup run had boosted the club's coffers, with victories over Uxbridge (by 8-0, an all-time record F.A.Cup win for the club), Oxford City (again) and Wycombe Wanderers, before a final intermediate round match against Plymouth Argyle. Just one step away from the entry of the "big boys", 10,000 spectators (gate money of £272) crammed into the York Road enclosure on the 16th of December for the match against Plymouth Argyle. Despite taking a goal lead before half-time, the visitors equalised, and in the replay at Home Park, Brentford were well beaten by 4-1. But the supporters were not too dismayed, and a few days later, on Boxing Day, the Southern League derby match at home to Fulham produced an all-time record York Road crowd of over 12,000 who paid record receipts of £345.

On Saturday the 2nd of April, Brentford played their last Southern League match at York Road, when they entertained Southampton. The match was lost 1-0, but the crowd numbering about 8,000 once again illustrated firstly how far the club had come in such a short time, and secondly their need for a suitable size enclosure. Two days later the final curtain came down on the Cricket Ground for the B's when Plymouth Argyle won this Western League game by the same scoreline.

There was no doubt that Brentford F.C. had by now become the premier sporting organisation in the district yet they were reliant on their "junior" hosts, the Boston Park Cricket Club, which included a restriction on the football playing season. Behind the scenes the quest for a permanent residence that the B's could truly called 'home' had not ceased, but during the season, the Club's Directors announced that their search was over, for a suitable site had been found – Griffin Park.

Chapter Two

A HOME AT LAST

After all the traumas of the first fifteen years of the club's life, and the moves to generally unsuitable home venues, a perfect site was found, no more than a hefty goalkick away from the Boston Park Cricket Ground. The site, an orchard owned by the nearby Chiswick brewers, Fuller, Smith and Turner, was conveniently located within the boundaries of Ealing Road, Braemar Road, New Road and Brook Road South. Convenient, for it was on the main tram (later bus) route to Ealing and Kew, and well within the boundaries of Brentford itself; in fact the club was literally coming home, for after fifteen years they had virtually completed the circle, for the west end of the ground was only about 100 metres from the pitch of their first home of Clifden House.

Griffin Park, as it became known, was acquired with the help of the Fulham Chairman Mr. Norris, a wealthy estate agent - and was initially offered to the Club to buy outright for £5,000. This sum was way beyond their means, but with the additional involvement of Brentford manager Richard Molyneux and club President Edwin Underwood, the Club were offered a very good alternative whereby they would occupy the ground on a 21-year lease at a very reasonable £40 per annum per acre. The club also had the option to buy the freehold from the owners at any time during this period, and still at the original price.

Possession of the ground was taken in early January 1904, and after the removal of gypsies who had decided to camp there, the process of changing a five-acre orchard site of around 200 trees into a professional football ground got underway. The initial intention was to provide not only a substantial football stadium, but probably to also ingratiate themselves with their neighbours, the additional facilities for bowls, cricket, tennis and other sports, complete with a cinder track and a final ground capacity for 35,000. These other pursuits of course never came to pass. The first task was to clear the orchard, and this was done virtually free of charge when the public were invited to undertake the work, and in lieu of payment were able to take away the felled timber for firewood.

Messrs John Russell of Haverstock Hill were appointed to undertake the levelling and turfing at Griffin Park, which commenced on the 24th of January, before they moved over to Shepherds Bush F.C. where they set about doing the same at the new ground of this local club; the ground in question was Loftus Road. Although the occupation of Loftus Road by Queens Park Rangers was to follow some years later, in fact these now two famous grounds - located just a few miles distance - were both opened within a month of each other. Just to complete a trio of moves, Queens Park Rangers themselves, who had been playing

Brentford's Ne

An invitation wa the Brentford direc rately view the clu number· accepted tl Fleet Street exclude cepting Mr. Lewis's c made to induce the Brentford to subscrib shares of 10s. each. benefits materially in m the presence of the clu experience no difficulty tional support they desi to boom as much in Br metropolitan districts, an a better conception of th ball Press than other club acknowledged, I am infor at the little luncheon w arranged for at the conc inspection. The Brentfore sided, made a speech that the course of which he c efforts made to further the p ciation game in the South which will be known as G capable of accommodating ne at present the wish of the B to provide comfort for 20,00 public inspection to-morrow playing pitch presents a fine and the system of drainage up-to-date principles. The sta tion, too, is most extensive, a size of the crowd, the onlooker an uninterrupted view of the p stands, dressing-rooms, pavilions approaching completion, and Griffen Park is admirably suita purposes.

*   *   *

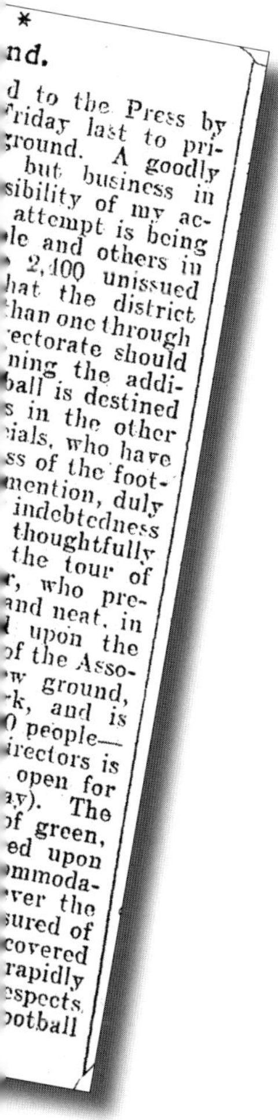

at Kensal Rise, also moved in 1904 to an alternative venue, to the agricultural showground that was located at Park Royal. Appointed in overall charge of the Griffin Park project were the Architects Parr and Kates.

While work continued, a public meeting was called at the Vestry Hall on the 11th of May with the intention of the disposal of the remaining shares. The total costs of the project were estimated at a modest - even for this period - £1,200. A packed Hall heard the club's President Mr. Underwood remind them of the great strides the club had made in the fifteen years of the club's existence. He informed those present that the Directors had received much support from the ground's owners, Messrs. Fuller Smith and Turner, and how valuable such open spaces were to local people. Despite the enthusiasm of the club members and followers, they were not so forthcoming with their pounds as they were with their non-financial support for the team. It must have been disappointing for Mr Underwood and the directors when only £300 was forthcoming, but having gone so far the club were determined to carry on with their long term plans. It was therefore left to the Directors to dig down deep into their pockets and provide the extra capital.

On the same day the members of the press were invited to inspect the ground. They were generous with their praise for this new football venue. The writer from *The Sportsman* enthused that: *"The improvements on the new ground are not yet complete, but when they are the enclosure will be one of the best appointed in the South of England."* The West London Football Review, commented upon Griffin Park: *"This name has been given to the new home, which is a vast improvement on the old ground."*

By now the pitch had been levelled, but with a slight camber in the centre, with a view to better drainage of the site, a factor which paid off in the many years to come. Three sides - Ealing Road, New Road and Brook Road - were elevated with the laying and compacting of ash, much of which came from a barge that had sunk in the nearby Thames. Some of the ash, or clinker as it was also known, was topped with timber to in effect provide terrace steps. This ensured that in wet weather the surface would drain through the ash layer.

As a cost cutting exercise the club employees, including the manager Mr. Molyneux, undertook much of the work. *"Thanks to the management, one of the finest playing pitches.... huge banking at the ends and part of the sides will enable many thousands to witness the game in comfort,"* said the man from the West London Football Review.

Frantic activity preceded the 1904/05 season. The stands that

Above: How the *West London Football Chat* described the new ground on May 10th 1904.

[Newspaper clipping fragment, left margin:]

nd.

d to the Press by 'riday last to pri- ground. A goodly but business in sibility of my ac- ·le and others in 2,400 unissued hat the district ·han one through ·ectorate should ning the addi- ball is destined s in the other ·ials, who have ss of the foot- ·mention, duly indebtedness thoughtfully the tour of ·, who pre- ·and neat. in upon the of the Asso- ·w ground, ·k, and is 0 people— ·rectors is open for ·y). The of green, ed upon ·mmoda- ·ver the ·ured of covered rapidly ·spects ·ootball

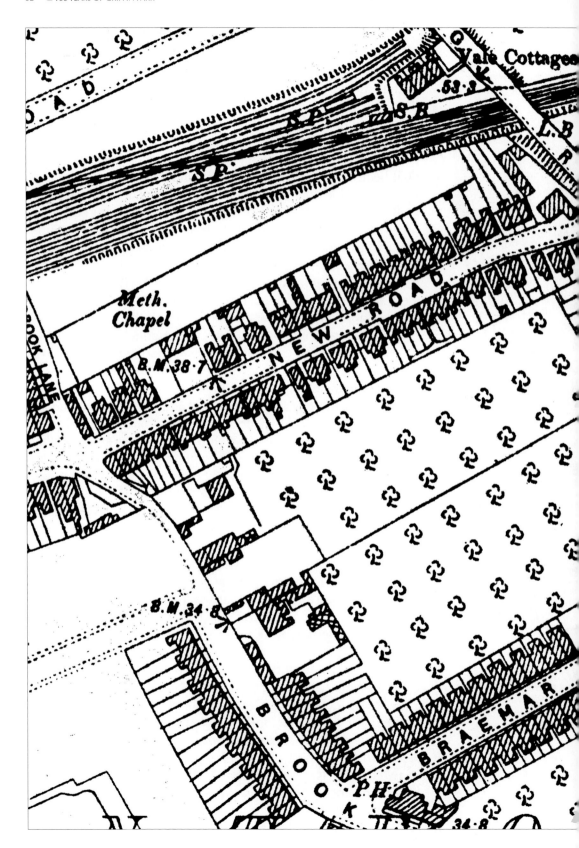

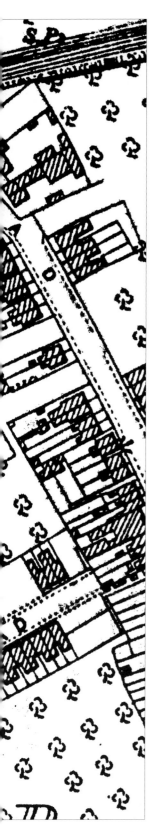

were owned by the football club were dismantled and moved the short distance to Griffin Park and were re-built. The "Flower Pot" stands were located at the back of the New Road terrace, which it was estimated would give standing cover for 2,000. The seated stand ran along two-thirds of the Braemar Road side. What the "Flower Pot" stands' were has never been determined. Possibly they were no more than small flimsy roofed and backed enclosures, which in any event only graced Griffin Park for a short time. The pitch enclosure fencing was also removed from the cricket ground and relocated, being set about one metre back from the playing area. The seating arrangements were inadequate, therefore a large addition to the old stand was built alongside, which provided seats for 1,500 in total, and stretched about two thirds the length of that side, with the intention that this would later be extended to full pitch length.

A relatively modest 20,000 capacity ground was aimed for although should support dictate it, this could be increased to thirty or even forty thousand. The turfs were laid and by the beginning of the summer the grass had already been cut several times. The pitch sized 110 yards by 73 was adequate, and in fact was both slightly longer and wider than that at York Road.

Initially entrance pay boxes were installed on three sides of the ground, via two entrances at each, although many years later the acquisition of two houses in New Road (numbers 62 and 63) allowed the fourth side to be added; a relatively rare example where all four sides of a football ground provides access and exits. The New Road side was expected to finally provide total standing for up to 10,000 spectators. The original intention was also to provide further cover on the Ealing Road end.

One factor that has made Griffin Park unique - by natural circumstances rather than by design - is the location of a Public House on each corner of the ground. At the Brook Road South and Braemar Road junction there is 'The Griffin' which has historic significance to the club, and at the opposite junction of Brook Road and New Road is the smaller "Royal Oak" - in fact the latter pub has been 'designated' by many to become the reference name referring to this end of the ground, i.e. "The Royal Oak

Left: Griffin Park in 1896, an orchard surrounded by victorian terrace houses. Note that Braemar Road is a cul-de-sac.

End". Where New Road meets Ealing Road, tucked in alongside the steep embankment leading to the railway bridge is "The New Inn", and finally where Ealing Road meets Braemar Road is "The Princess Royal".

The Braemar Road side from the initial days was to become the main hub of the club, but it also provided problems at the outset. The development of this side was undertaken in a great rush, and at a minimum cost. In depth the wooden Stands (both old and new) had around eight rows with a standing paddock area in front for around four rows. This left a reasonable space behind for the provision of a collection of small structures, including separate dressing rooms for both teams and the match officials (including bathrooms), a recreation area for the team and various other offices.

On the 20th of July, the grand opening of Griffin Park went off in a somewhat deflated fashion. The Grand Sports Meeting programme scheduled had to be downgraded, when the Amateur Athletics Association refused permission for its members to take part, as they frowned upon the venue, as it was that of a professional football club. Then the Football Association forbade the club from holding a giant lottery at the ground, which promised the addition of more much needed funds. Despite these setbacks the day attracted between two to three thousand to Griffin Park, where the afternoon started musically with an appearance by the Brentford Gasworks Band. Fairground swings and roundabouts provided other entertainment, but the day only raised a paltry £25 profit.

On the 16th of August, "Uncle Boffin" in *"The Football Chat"* enthused: *"Very few grounds in London, if any, are better* (than Griffin Park). *The new Stand, which is nearing completion has a 700 capacity, whilst the already erected old stand can seat 1000 plus."*

Below: December 1904, just a few months after the opening of Griffin Park. This composite picture shows the extent of the former Boston Park Cricket Ground stand and the slight change of roof construction where the new extension continued.

Over 140,000 attended Brentford's first team matches in the previous 1903/04 season, and this support was expected to continue following the sale of season tickets which exceeded the numbers for any preceding season, and indeed were supposedly soon sold out. These tickets were well priced at ten shillings (50p) for the ground only and twenty-one shillings (£1-05) for the stand and enclosures - cheaper in fact than any other Southern League club. But this "sell-out" was something of an exaggeration, for just before the first match, it was announced that just one ticket was left. This would be given free to the first letter opened on Wednesday 31st August, providing the return postage cost of one guinea (£1-05) was enclosed. Even so it was soon found necessary to print more season tickets.

A handbook was also printed for the first time and this indeed soon sold out. Despite the building of the offices at Griffin Park, the Princess Royal Hotel was listed as the club's headquarters, and it was from here that the season tickets had been on sale from the Secretary/Manager Mr Molyneux. Prior to the start of the season, on the 20th August (and again a week later) a large number of amateurs were given their opportunity to impress with two trial matches at Griffin Park. On the latter date around 3,000 spectators were present, when the 'Whites' beat the 'Stripes' 4-2. The entrance charge to see these matches was just one penny, with this gate money passed on to local charities.

Many new players, especially forwards, were signed-on prior to the start of the new season, including Hobson (from West Bromwich Albion), Boag and Warrington (from Derby County), former Southampton player Oliver, Walker from Scotland and - soon to be - Irish International Tommy Shanks returned from Woolwich Arsenal after less than two years away following his record £200 transfer to the then South London club. £600 had been raised to pay the summer wages, and the club looked

The Council's Surveyor's fears regarding the safety of the Braemar Road stand when it was rebuilt at the opening of Griffin Park in 1904 was somewhat vindicated when much of the roof was blown off during a gale a few months later in January 1905. Considerable damage was caused to several houses backing on to the ground in Braemar Road.

hopefully forward to a successful season.

Such had been the haste to complete the facilities that the seated stand addition was only completed on the morning of the inaugural Griffin Park football match on the 1st September. This match, on a Thursday (the first day of September was the traditional first day of the season at this time), saw a Western League fixture, the opponents being Plymouth Argyle.

With little sympathy for the club, the Borough Surveyor who by law had to give official approval - stunned the club when he declared the Stand was unsafe. Two days later, the local council minutes expressed doubts with regard to its safety. This opinion was disputed by the *West London Football Review*, who commented that the stand: " *resting on a huge concrete floor supported with huge iron girders appeared strong enough."* In addition the Surveyor refused to sanction the use of the dressing rooms until certain modification and improvements were carried out. The club had no choice to comply, and there was the anti-climax whereby the two teams had to change at the public baths a few hundred metres away, then walk down Clifden Road, before making a somewhat inglorious entrance onto the pitch. However, according to the *West London Football Review* again, the players appreciated the opportunity for a swim!

But the supporters were not to be deterred, and the attendance on that memorable day numbered over 4,000. The second home

Left: The oldest known Brentford home programme, a Southern league Fixture against Bristol Rovers in September 1904.

Report of the Works Committee dated 23rd August, 1904.

Your Committee having considered the plans presented by the Brentford Football Club recommend that the same be formally disapproved, the building shewn not being intended to be constructed in accordance with the Bye-Laws.

WILLIAM BRADLEY,
Chairman.

Above: An extract from Brentford Urban District Council's minutes during August 1904 relating to the prevention of use of the Braemar Road stand.

Southern League game on the 17th of September brought Bristol Rovers to Griffin Park, and the stand and press box were used for the first time. There was a reasonable crowd of 6,000 present, when the ground was described by one newspaper as being, *"a compact enclosure."* A one-goal defeat ensued, although it was generally agreed that the B's were unlucky in this game. In fact it wasn't until the visit of Portsmouth two weeks later that the first Brentford Southern League goal was scored, by Warrington.

A telephone line was installed at Griffin Park in October, and at the ground, pictures of two Brentford heroes - Tommy Shanks and George Parsonage - were on sale.

The highlight of the season came in the F.A.Cup when the team reached the intermediate round for the third season running. This followed a controversial and bad tempered victory over Queens Park Rangers, and included a sending-off in the match at Park Royal, which was an almost unheard of event at this period. Reading were now the visitors, and the match attracted previously unprecedented interest. The capacity of Griffin Park was tested with an attendance of around 16,000 who paid £521. Leading by a single goal, the B's looked like reaching the first round proper for the first time, but a controversial penalty a minute from time gave the Berkshire team a goal, and they duly won the replay.

The season ended with the runners-up spot in the Western League, but - in spite of high expectations - a lowly 14th of 18 in the Southern. Once again, the supporters remained faithful with attendances normally between six and eight thousand, and up to 12,000 for the visit of Fulham. But the wage bill that had soared by 30% to £3,490 wasn't fully recouped in gate money that only rose by 26%, to £4,171. However, the club had reasonable cause to feel optimistic about the future after this, their first season at their new home.

The next campaign started in a better vein than a year earlier, and after just a few games the Bees were up near the top of the table. The crowds again averaged around the six to eight thousand

A Southern League encounter between Brentford and Fulham at Griffin Park on the 7th of October 1905.

mark, but it was the local derby matches that proved to be the real money-spinners. The best league crowd of the season was for the visit of Fulham in October when 15,000 packed into Griffin Park, and just a thousand less two months later when Tottenham Hotspur were the visitors.

For the first time, Brentford reached the Third Round proper of the F.A. Cup. The club entered at the fourth qualifying stage when they easily overcame the amateurs of Wycombe Wanderers by 4-0 before a 5,000 Griffin Park attendance. There was now no intermediate stage round, and therefore the team progressed through to the first round where they played runaway Second Division leaders Bristol City, again at home. The attendance of 12,000 was somewhat disappointing, but the result wasn't for Brentford won 2-1 after being a goal down at half time. Without doubt this was the club's greatest achievement to date, although it did tend to confirm that the gap between the Southern League and the Football League was not so great as might have been expected. And this surmise was emphasised in the next round.

Another Second Division side were the next visitors in the Cup, mid-table Lincoln City, and they were comfortably brushed aside, losing 3-0, but before a very disappointing crowd of only 9,000. But the Bees were brought down to earth in the 3rd round, at which stage there were just sixteen teams left in the competition. Drawn away to First Division leaders - and eventual Champions - Liverpool, they were no match for the Merseyside team, losing by a 2-0 scoreline.

Tragedy struck at the season's end. Secretary/Manager Dick Molyneux who had transformed the club on the field, after returning from a serious operation in January was unable to continue his duties and he was released from his contract. In early June he returned home to Liverpool, but within a few days died. It is impossible to say whether Brentford's plight in the next

Left: A view of the crowd on the Brook Road (ash and clinker) terrace for the F.A.Cup-tie against Preston. Note the large 'advert' for the Supporters League that had been formed in September, just a few months earlier.

few years would still have come to pass if it had not been for the untimely death of the manager. Things had perhaps already made a turn for the worse, but after Brentford stalwart William Brown was appointed to lead the Bees the situation was eventually to deteriorate. Brown was an accomplished administrator, but not a football manager.

During the summer, the Brentford Baseball Club used the ground for three years from 1908. Baseball became a fairly popular off-season sport at many football clubs for a few years, having been inaugurated in England back in 1890 by four leading Football League clubs. This latter use of Griffin Park produced around £50 per season, and collectively these extra activities raised well over £300, which at this time was an appreciable sum.

The Directors had at one time seriously considered moving to the newly-built White City Stadium for home matches, although this would appear to have been ill conceived for this was on the doorstep of Queens Park Rangers and increased crowds were unlikely. In fact three years later the Rangers played two well attended Southern League matches at the Stadium.

In August 1910, it was reported that at Griffin Park, *the "turf is good, and the stands have been freshly painted."* The Bees started that season in good form, and in September the Brentford Supporters League was formed, the club's first ever supporters club. The aim of the league was twofold - raise funds for the parent club and to encourage support at away matches. In the case of the latter they organised for around 500 supporters to travel by special train to Northampton on Boxing Day. Brentford were riding high in third place, but the Cobblers - in sixth - won 2-0. In the return match the following May there was an almost unprecedented crowd numbering 13,770 - the biggest attendance for three years - but a disappointing draw was the result. A few weeks later the team exited the F.A.Cup, unluckily losing to Preston North End by 1-0, the only bright spot being another 14,000 crowd.

Below: The 14th of January 1911, and the visit of Preston North End in the F.A.Cup, which attracted a record (at the time) Griffin Park crowd of 14,000. Although of poor quality, this illustrates the substantial open banking (to the left) of the Brook Road end.

Left: Although not entirely relevant to Brentford F.C. (These two teams are those of the "T" Division Metropolitan Police and the Brentford Special Constabulary), this photograph provides a rare sight of the old Braemar Road stand and the open Brook Road end at Christmas 1915.

The end of season run was poor, the team winning just two matches in the last 16, due in the main to an injury spell, and from 5th place they ended in a lowly 12th. This year saw the first annual match versus Queens Park Rangers staged to raise funds for the King Edward VII Hospital in Ealing. Brentford won this inaugural match 4-0, the event raised £40, and for the second time in their history, a match involving the club at Griffin Park was filmed.

By the start of the First World War, Griffin Park itself received little attention simply because the continual hard times prevented very little in the way of improvements to the ground. It was still virtually unchanged since its inauguration, the only particularly notable difference being the apparent early disappearance of the enigmatic "Flower Pot Stands' on the New Road side embankment. The few pre-1915 photographs portraying this area do not show

Below: An aerial view where match action can be seen at Griffin Park (Near top, off centre to the right). The road leading from the church (bottom of the photograph) to the ground being Layton Road

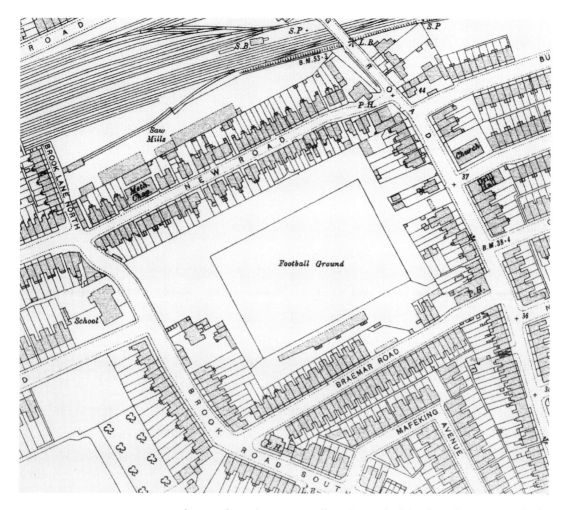

any form of enclosure at all. It is probable that these were little more than elongated timber and corrugated iron roofed sheds that very soon after their installation at Griffin Park were demolished. On the Braemar Road side of the ground there was the near full length seated stand with a paddock area in front. However this was considerably narrower than the latter, and present, stand. At both ends of the ground, as with the New Road side, there were just earth and ash embankments. No doubt in the modern safety of grounds considerations, they would be considered highly dangerous, especially in wet weather when it can be assumed they became somewhat messy slippery slopes. Although not recorded, it would seem that from studying the photographs of 1905 and 1922, the New Road banking was in fact increased in depth between these dates.

Brentford had come a long way in their near 26 years of existence, the last eleven at Griffin Park. Much of their success, even if the last few years had been a struggle, could be attributed

Above: A map of Griffin Park in 1915, nine years after the Club made it their home. Braemar Road is now open at both ends with houses now built to the east of Ealing road. These were demolished fifty years later.

to the founders of the club, a few of whom were still associated with it. Not least of these patrons was Edwin Underwood, a faithful supporter and benefactor who had done so much for the Bees in the early days. On the 6th of March 1915, near The Beehive public house and outside his office, he was tragically run over by a car (an extremely rare accident at this time) and died. He was 76 years of age.

There was to be one more season of Southern League football before the club's "promotion", but at least they were elected to the enlarged First Division, along with the Welsh contingent of Merthyr Town, Swansea Town and Newport County. With the difficulty of obtaining the necessary materials, and a year of what was seen as consolidation after the hostilities, the expected ground improvements had to wait. It was recognised by the club in the 1919-20 season handbook that the facilities were far from good: *"Our Stand accommodation was found to be quite inadequate to cope with the numbers who wanted a seat. It is to be regretted that for this season it has not been found possible to rebuild or enlarge the Stand, but we are quite expecting that before long something very substantial may be done to provide more seating accommodation."*

The time factor referred to in fact stretched to eight long years before a decent stand worthy of the club saw the light of day. But changes inevitably were made in the playing personnel, particularly with some pre-war players now retired, and others sadly who lost their lives fighting for their country. The cost to watch a first team game at Griffin Park for the coming season

Below: The New Road side during the Middlesex Charity Cup final between Botwell Mission (later Hayes) and Golders Green (later Hendon). Compare this photograph with that of 1905 taken from a similar viewpoint. Between times it would appear that the banking had been raised.

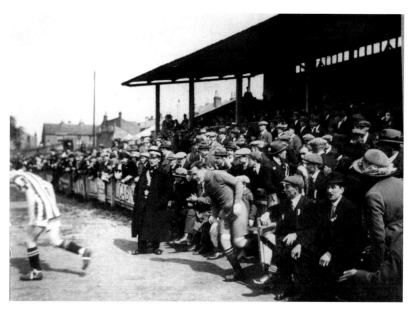

Right: The two teams come out for the 1922 Middlesex Charity Cup Final at Griffin Park. A fine view of the east end of the "Cow Shed" (seated stand) and the undeveloped area next to the Ealing Road end.

was for adults one shilling (5p), and one shilling and sixpence (7.5p) for the enclosure, or two shillings for the Stand. Boys were approximately half these prices. Southern League rules insisted however that ladies and soldiers pay full price.

An enthusiastic crowd numbering around 12,000 was present for the first match of the 1919/20 season, at Griffin Park, when Brighton and Hove Albion were beaten 2-1. Two days later, and again at home, the numbers dropped - to 8,000 for the visit of Millwall.

On the field it was not a particularly successful campaign, with the team finishing 15th of 22nnd, but despite the euphoric previous season, this was one of consolidation. However, peacetime crowds were up, with eight to ten thousand at Griffin Park being normal, with two exceptions when Q.P.R. were the visitors on Boxing Day when the Bees won 2-1, and 14,220 turned up. Conversely the last home game, when Exeter City were the visitors, the numbers slumped to 3,000. However, the most significant event of the season occurred on the 18th of May in Sheffield, when a meeting between the Football and the Southern Leagues resulted in at last an extension of the premier competition. Starting in time for the 1920/21 season, a new Third Division was created from the Southern League First Division, whose members were voted in en bloc.

Efforts to improve the facilities at Griffin Park during the summer of 1920 became a priority. The Press had already complained about their facilities during the previous season, and their requirements were easily fulfilled, with the provision of a *"cosy little structure at the rear of the old stand"*, complete with two telephones for their use.

Despite the hoped for Stand improvements promised a year earlier, these did not materialise, and it was to be several years before they appeared. But £2,000 was spent elsewhere, principally on the uncovered New Road side. This first proper terracing, in concrete (presumably incorporated with railway sleepers), was installed on the "popular" (New Road) side, with thirty steps and complete with gangways, but developments at each end of the ground had to be put on hold. The New Road side improvements required 1760 loads of earth and 1,240 railway sleepers.

With the club still in debt this improvement was probably all that could reasonably be expected, but at least the standing spectator could hope for dry feet - even if his head got wet.

Other expenditure was made on obtaining the services of eleven new players, but as it turned out this was proved to be a poor investment. Season Tickets were priced at seventeen shillings (85p) for the ground only, and twice this price to sit. The season started disappointedly with a 3-0 defeat at Exeter, and two days later, on the 30th of August Griffin Park hosted its first Football League match. Brentford's form in their First League season was generally poor, with mostly defeats, and by the end of November, the crowd had slumped to 6,000 for Reading's visit.

The visit of Huddersfield Town in the F.A.Cup produced a fillip, when 14,892 turned out to see the visitors narrowly win by the odd goal in three. A big improvement from a year earlier, when, against the same opponents - but played in Yorkshire - The Bees lost 5-1. The season finished most disappointingly with the team languishing second from bottom, and having to apply for re-election at the end of this, the first season of the Third Division. Their fate, however, could have been worse, for at one time the League Management Committee was considering reducing the division's numbers that could have spelt the end of the club at this level.

In the final event, the Bees fortunes were not in danger, for it was agreed that it would be unfair to consider voting out the two

Below: Training at Griffin Park in August 1922. An excellent view of the junction of Braemar Road and Ealing Road, at this time devoid of any cover. The Braemar Road stand did not extend the full length of this side, whilst the irregular 'hump' that comprised the Ealing Road embankment had just the occasional crash barrier.

bottom clubs - Gillingham were also handed the wooden spoon - after just one season, and no voting took place. Newcomers that summer were Charlton Athletic and Aberdare Athletic who replaced promoted Crystal Palace and Grimsby Town who moved into the newly formed Third Division North; the Third Division, after one year became the Third Division South.

Whilst the club retained its status, there was hardly cause for celebration, for an enormous £1,555 was lost on the season, which resulted in a total debt of nearly £6,000. Yet the attendances were reasonable, with an average for League games of 8,660, albeit the eighth worst in the whole Football League (Reading were bottom of the list with an average of 7,150, whilst the division's top club for support was Millwall with nearly 19,000). Three Directors resigned, and those that were left decided that it was time to appoint a full time Manager - Fred Halliday had up to that time concentrated more on the administrative side of things - in line with most other professional clubs.

It came as no surprise when there was a mass clearout of players, and with renewed optimism that greets every new season, with which every football supporter is familiar, success was predicted for the new look Bees. However, before a Griffin Park crowd of nearly 12,000, visitors Merthyr Town went back to South Wales with two points. The early season matches continued in a poor way, and when Charlton Athletic made their first ever visit to Griffin Park, before a healthy 13,000 attendance,

Right: High kicking from Harry Morris, in August 1922. A good view can be seen of the Braemar Road seated stand - the "Cow Shed" - which provided the only cover at the ground at this time. To the right, the open Brook Road end.

apart from another Bees defeat, crowd problems added to the club's misfortunes. A spectator ran on to the pitch and assaulted a visiting player, whilst fighting on the terraces proved that such incidents were not a new phenomenon when they were extensively reported some fifty years later.

But there then came a dramatic improvement in the results, and a good F.A. Cup run saw the famous Tottenham Hotspur as visitors to Griffin Park in the third round. Anticipating a new record attendance, the Board decided to cash in on the event and doubled the normal admission price to one shilling (5p). But the plan backfired, for the fans outraged at this increase boycotted the game in their thousands. Only 12,964 were present to see the illustrious visitors come away with the expected victory. Even so, the match did produce new record gate receipts of £1,488.

The 21-year lease on Griffin Park had by now come to an end but any hope of purchasing the site for £5,000 (the 1904 figure that remained in force) was completely out of the question, as indeed it had been during the interim period; the club had

Left: George Kell. The 1924/25 season, just prior to the adoption of the now famous red and white striped shirts. George is standing in front of the original Braemar Road stand. Although the much maligned "Cow Shed" had been at Griffin Park for 20 years, this timber structure still looked in reasonable condition. Note the wooden terraced paddock area in front of the seating portion.

enough trouble raising £200 for the annual rent. But Landlords Fullers proved themselves to be true friends to the football club, and agreed to extend the lease for another eight years, with the ongoing proviso that it could still be bought outright for £5,000 during the interim period.

The Directors resolved to make available *"a substantial sum of money"* to improve the playing side of affairs with one last ditch effort, recognising that any repeats of the previous season's disaster would surely spell the end of the club. Just two players were re-signed for the 1925/26 season, but there was one dramatic change, that of the team colours. From their white shirts and black shorts, the team strip was changed to the now familiar red and white striped shirts and black shorts; with the exception of just one season these colours have remained constant to the present day.

Claiming just one point in the first ten games, by mid-October Brentford were rooted firmly at the bottom of the table. But apart from the results there were other problems too. On the 12th of September the club entertained Brighton and Hove Albion before a 7,000 crowd. Disputed goals by both sides led to ill feeling between the players and this rubbed off on the crowd who yelled abuse - and orange peel - at the opposition players, and then

Below: The successful 1926-27 team that reached the Fifth Round of the F.A. Cup, which significantly helped to pay for the new Braemar Road stand.

the referee. Brentford's Jack Allen was sent off after a particularly bad foul, which led to further unrest from the crowd. Brighton meanwhile added to their goal tally, finally running out 6-1 winners. At the end of the match they and the match officials had to make a hasty retreat from the pitch, pursued by hundreds of irate home fans. Appeals for calm went unheeded, and eventually police reinforcements were called for. It came as no surprise that the incident was reported to the Football League and the outcome was the closure of Griffin Park for fourteen days.

Therefore the next "home" match was not played at Griffin Park, and instead of entertaining Crystal Palace the fixtures were reversed, with The Bees travelling to Selhurst Park three weeks later, where they lost 2-0. When all seemed lost a reasonable recovery followed, aided in no small way with the acquisition of Ernie Watkins from Southend United in early January for a record Brentford transfer fee. The team underwent a reasonable revival which gradually lifted them from the lower reaches of the table, apart from a final poor run-in, although they drew with promotion contenders Plymouth Argyle in the last home match, before a surprisingly good crowd of around 12,000, the best for nearly three years.

The final outcome was a final fifth from bottom in the League table, well clear in places from re-election, but notably only three points above second from bottom Charlton Athletic; local rivals Queens Park Rangers were bottom with a meagre 21 points, fourteen less than Charlton. Whilst Brentford's revival was hardly that of great proportions, their revival at the gate was, for during the season the average attendance rose to an incredible 9,146 - their best ever - and the sixth best in the division. This success was attributed to a team that played attractive football, even if the results did not always produced

Below: A programme for a Baseball game staged at Griffin Park in 1923. The Heinz team spent a successful three years at Brentford between 1908 and 1911.

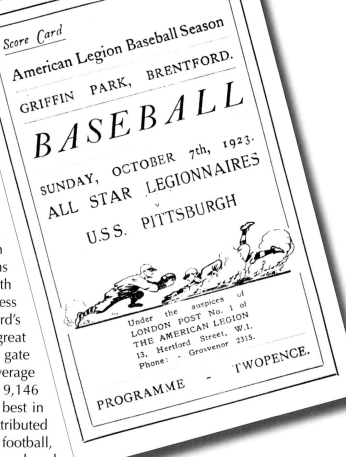

Score Card

American Legion Baseball Season

GRIFFIN PARK, BRENTFORD.

BASEBALL

SUNDAY, OCTOBER 7th, 1923.

ALL STAR LEGIONNAIRES

U.S.S. PITTSBURGH

Under the auspices of
LONDON POST No. 1 of
THE AMERICAN LEGION
13, Hertford Street, W.1.
Phone: - Grosvenor 2315.

PROGRAMME - TWOPENCE.

the desired outcome.

At last the club had good reason to look forward to the future with optimism, not least with the appointment of a new manager in Harry Curtis, the former referee. With only nine players retained, Curtis - with a very limited budget - sought to improve his squad and signed two from Scottish Junior football, whilst six newcomers made their way from Gillingham, the manager's previous club. The core of the previous team remained, including cricketer Patsy Hendren, Ernie Watkins and the two Jacks - Allen and Lane.

After the poor start of a year earlier, the 1926/27 season started in complete contrast, and following the beating of Brighton 4-0 in the opening game (before a 12,000 Griffin Park crowd), three more victories followed, and despite a defeat during this period, this opening run took the team to the top of the table for the first time ever. Even better was to follow, for the next week a 4-2 win over Queens Park Rangers, not only consolidated their position but also attracted a new record League attendance of 19,380 to Griffin Park. The fans packed the old and by now somewhat dilapidated stand, whilst the majority crammed onto the largely inadequate, and unprotected from the elements, slopes on the two ends of the ground, although others at least had cover over the concrete terrace steps they stood on, on the New Road side.

An indifferent run over the ensuing months resulted in a gradual slide down the table, but a prolonged F.A. Cup run lifted the supporters' spirits. Non-League Clapton were first easily overcome (but only after a replay), followed by Gillingham - after another replay - and Oldham athletic. The latter tie also took two efforts to resolve, following abandonment due to bad light at the first attempt. Now through to the fourth round, a draw was achieved at First Division West Ham United, and the Hammers were beaten 2-0 in the replay. The Griffin Park attendance was 20,799.

This exciting cup run resulted in a poor end of season record in the League, for the last ten games produced not one victory - but only three defeats. The final table showed Brentford in a satisfactory, if somewhat disappointing mid-table position, but at least with a healthy Bank balance on the season. The cup run of course added to the income enormously, but so did the Griffin Park League gates that rose to nearly 10,000. Further income came via the transfer fees received for the sale of Allen, Anderson and Archie Clark, and at long last the Board felt the time had come, and the finance to pay for it, for a major ground improvement at Griffin Park.

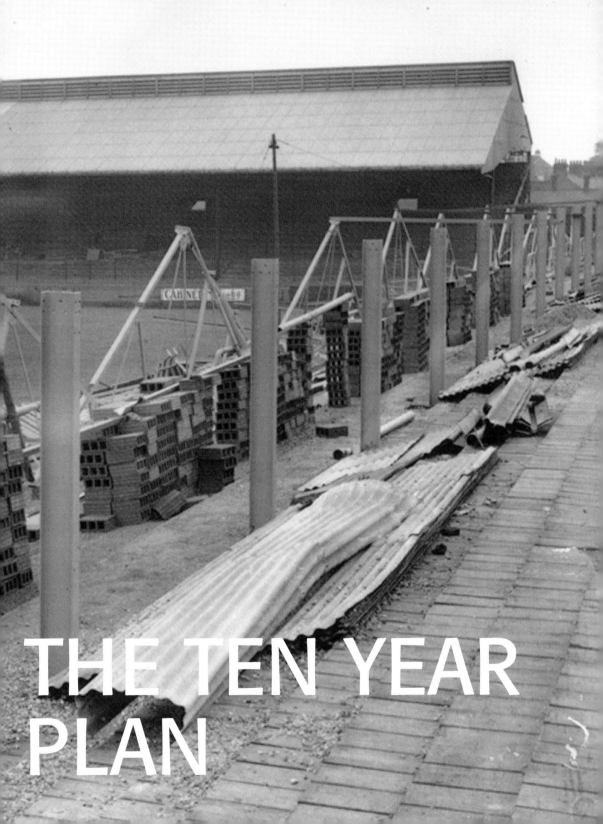

Chapter Three

THE TEN YEAR PLAN

The old "Cow Shed" stand on the Braemar Road side had withstood the weather for around thirty years and had also been transferred (from the Boston Park Cricket Ground). Now at last it was decided to demolish the structure and build in its place a brand new pitch length seated stand. As soon as it became apparent that sufficient funds would be available, planning permission was sought, and on approval, work started in great haste during the close season. The impressive new stand, constructed of timber, steel and concrete, provided seating for around 3,500 with covered standing on the several steps of concrete paddock in front.

This project, which was completed in time for the opening home match of the 1927/28 season, cost around £5,000. It was formally opened by the F.A. Secretary Sir Frederick Wall before the first home match of the season against Northampton Town. The club was still in debt and had to rely on a bank overdraft, but at least a substantial proportion of this sum had been paid for from the financial rewards of the previous season. It now remained for the Bees to justify the confidence and bold move made by the club. Typically the team got the season off to a bad start, losing 5-2 at Brighton, but redeemed themselves with a good run into October. But the season became one of inconsistency including a dreadful sequence of results in December and most of January. As promotion thoughts rapidly faded the supporters deserted the club in droves.

On December the 5th, when Walsall were the visitors, the attendance of 2,202 (this is the official figure reported to the Football League, most sources give 2,024) has gone down in the record books as Brentford's lowest Football League gate to

Below: The 1929-30 team that won twenty-one home games in a row - a feat as yet unbeaten in football.

date; however, in fairness it has to be realised that this game was played on a Monday winter's afternoon (pre-floodlights), and just before Christmas. Ironically the club recorded a rare victory that day. On January the 28th, this time a Saturday, there were barely 3,000 at Griffin Park for Luton Town's visit. There was also no cup bonanza, for excluded until the Third Round this season; they were crushed at Old Trafford when Manchester United won 7-1.

The team's form picked up, and so did the gates for the remainder of the season, and at least they achieved a just below mid-table respectability. Over the season, the home attendances slumped to an average of 7,331. Despite now one of the better of Third Division grounds, there were fewer people visiting. But with some big money outgoing transfers, the club managed to balance the books, and it appears that all those involved with Brentford F.C. were still looking with confidence to the future.

The 1928/29 season got off to a fine start, with the team undefeated in the first seven games and every home game during this run attracting five figure gates, including a record League crowd of nearly 22,000 for Queen's Park Rangers' visit. Then, when promotion was being freely talked about, there was a dreadful slump playing wise, and just two points were obtained in the next 13 games, which now turned the Bees into re-election candidates.

True to character, winning ways returned after Christmas, and if it hadn't have been for an awful final run-in, with just one point from five matches, then a higher than 13th final place amongst 24 would have been realised. With a healthy overall rise in home attendances, the Directors showed their resolve and once again, despite the ongoing financial problems, spent quite freely on new players in an effort to realise their ambition - promotion. Who could have imagined what treats that would soon be in store for the Griffin Park supporters.

Aided notably by two of the new signings, Billy Lane (from Reading) and Cyril Blakemore (ex-Bristol City), the Bees started the 1929/30 season in fine form with a brace of home victories, first beating Swindon Town 3-2 and then - before a record midweek crowd of around 21,000 - overcoming the challenge of newly relegated Clapton Orient, with a 3-1 scoreline. By mid-October, the team had only suffered one defeat, and in the ten matches just two draws. Promotion was on the lips of everybody at Griffin Park, but of course how often had they flattered to deceive. But the supporters were certainly confident, and as the victories built up, particularly a continuous run of home victories, so did the attendances.

Brentford and Plymouth Argyle were the front runners, the

latter being beaten early in the New Year before a 20,571 crowd, and the following month a similar figure (22,033) was repeated when Fulham visited Griffin Park on the 22nd, where the visitors were soundly beaten 5-1. If the home record was impeccable, the weak spot was the team's results on their travels, and a poor to modest set of results was to prove their undoing. On the 21st of April, local rivals Queens Park Rangers were easily beaten 3-0 in the last home match, but of particular relevance was that this created an unbeatable record in which Brentford had won all 21 home games. Yet early in April it took a 90th minute match-winning goal from John Payne to maintain this run, when Southend United were overcome 2-1 after the visitors were leading until the 77th minute. But unfortunately this achievement was insufficient to earn the club their cherished ambition of promotion, for the Devon club with seven points more, became the Champions, in these days when only one club could rise to the Second Division. The Bees' away form, which let them down, produced nine defeats and five drawn games.

It was a bitter disappointment, for in almost any other season, the Bees' 61 points would have been sufficient for promotion, but at least the fans recognised the team's efforts, and with an average attendance for League matches during the season of 12,123 this represented an almost 50% increase on the previous campaign. Now, into the 1930s, this decade was to prove the greatest in the Club's history. Perhaps sensing that they were on the verge of success, and aided by more money in the coffers, a major ground improvement was undertaken. The sloping and unsurfaced embankment behind the Ealing Road goal was concreted during the close season, to provide a large comfortable terrace, leaving just the opposite Brook Road end undeveloped.

It was a bitter disappointment when the team were thrashed 4-0 by Northampton at home in the opening fixture of the 1930/31 season following their sensational Griffin Park form in the previous campaign. Since they had also lost their last Griffin Park game of 1928/29, the run of League victories was confined just to that one complete season. Although they soon returned to their winning ways again, there was never any hope of even coming close to the home form of a year earlier. From early on, Notts County were the clear front-runners, and even after less than a third of the fixtures completed, they led the Bees by three places and eight points. This season saw a good F.A. Cup run, yet Brentford appeared at Wembley Stadium a week before their first round victory, when they played at the twin towers in a League match with Clapton Orient who were temporarily using the venue as a home ground.

Further Cup victories came over Norwich City and Cardiff City (after a replay), before the team bowed out at the 4th round stage by 1-0 at home to First Division Portsmouth before a record attendance of 23,544. By now, late January, the season was all but over, and honour was the only goal to fight for. The early season five figure crowds slumped to 8,000 for the last home match, versus Watford, and a final third place in the table had to suffice. Yet the runaway Champions Notts County, eight points ahead of second placed Crystal Palace, "only" amassed 59 points - two less than the Bees unsuccessful challenge of a year earlier.

The summer of 1931 saw the final side of Griffin Park - the Brook Road end - undergo development. Initially this was unroofed and limited to just concrete terracing, but the work undertaken provided a good standing bank behind that goal. Another major ground development during the summer was the oofing of the New Road side. It was a substantial cover in 1931, built upon proper roof trusses and included drainage. Griffin Park

Below: An aerial view of Griffin Park in 1931, showing the new concrete of the Ealing Road terrace. The Boston Park cricket ground can be seen at the top of the picture.

was now considered to one of the best grounds outside the First Division, and with the absolute capacity now having been raised to around 30,000.

The 1931/32 season got off in fine style with a 1-0 win over the team from Shepherds Bush, before a new record crowd of 25,000, although this figure only remained for a few months, for on Christmas Day a massive attendance of 26,741 (receipts of £1,733), saw Griffin Park literally bursting at the seams; a section of the railings at the Ealing Road end collapsed due to the pressure on them spilling out spectators onto the pitch surrounds. Fortunately there were no injuries.

After the opening victory there was a slight hiccup with only a draw at lowly Thames Association in East London (their second season of two in the League), and a defeat at Exeter City.

But further victories followed, and after eight matches the Bees were vieing with Southend United at the top of the table. Just before Christmas, following victory over Watford, Brentford were top, a fitting pairing with the reserve team who headed the London Combination, and who attracted a 4,500 attendance for the visit of Bournemouth. Half-way through the season the Bees travelled to Q.P.R's. ground - now based at the White City - where another victory ensued.

A good F.A.Cup run was terminated at Manchester City, where, before a 56,190 crowd that Bees were thrashed 6-1; poor for the morale but excellent for the bank balance. The match was filmed, and the highlights (or should it be lowlights) remain on record today. By now the team were faltering in their promotion challenge, and this continued before a final dreadful run-in to the end of the season that extinguished all hopes, when they could only manage two victories (the last games of the season) plus one

Below: A major development of Griffin Park, in the Summer of 1933, was the part covering of the deep concrete terraced Brook Road End (also later known as the Royal Oak end). The high rear entrances to the terrace were later changed and entry was gained at the lower level around halfway up

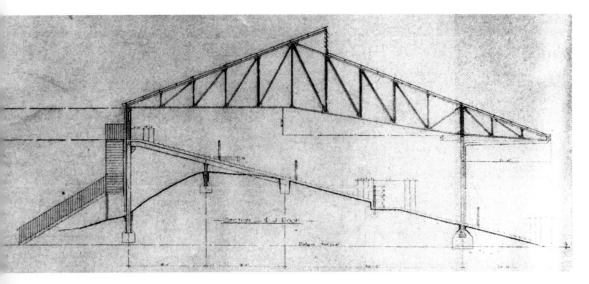

Right: Initially the vast Brook Road cover was somewhat ungainly as it only ran for half the width of the ground.

draw from their last ten games. It was a bitter disappointment for all at the club, with the crowds plunging to 7,000 for the last match (the last in the League for Thames), and a final fifth place in the table.

It was rumoured that Manager Harry Curtis had tendered his resignation, after five years at the helm, but this did not materialise, and in fact for the relatively paltry sum of £1,500 (that the club could scarcely afford, although the match receipts that season had been the highest ever), he signed three Middlesbrough reserve players. Jack Holliday, Billy Scott and Bert Watson were arguably the buy of the decade, as the trio were instrumental in lifting Brentford to the First Division.

The summer of 1932 was to signal the start of six seasons that produced unprecedented success for the Club. The team had opened up a seven-point lead at the table top by mid-November following a phenomenal start to the season, with seven straight wins, followed with two draws, and then another five victories. Following the last of these - in true storybook fashion - their first defeat came at Cardiff City - who were bottom of the table. The team's continual tenure at the top was rarely questioned, and with a final ten match unbeaten run (strangely the last three games were drawn) the team finished the season as Champions at last.

Their average attendance for the 1932/33 season of 13,300 was the highest in their division and better than over half of the teams in the Second, and four from the First. Even the reserve team could not be denied their moment of glory, for they captured the London Combination title for the second time in succession, sealing it with a 3-0 victory over Aldershot before a record crowd at this level of 9,000. The second eleven had just completed an amazing sequence of results which started on the 21st November 1931, and only ended nearly two years later, on the 4th of November 1933. During this long period, the team played 44 home games in the London Combination, and won every one, during which time they scored 159 goals and conceded just 23 - a record that even overshadowed that of the

Summer 1935, with workmen busy constructing the west wing of the Braemar Road stand.

first team's consecutive victories run.

It was clear that where possible further improvements had to be considered for Griffin Park. One of the biggest developments was the first stage in the enlargement of the Brook Road end. Until now, this had consisted of about twenty-five uncovered concrete terrace steps, but the embankment was substantially built up higher and a further batch of terrace steps added to bring the total to around 65 in total. A massive steel trussed roof was added, with an overhang that extended to the pitch line and spanning about 100 feet (30 metres). Yet this enormous new covered terrace for a short while looked quite ungainly as only half of the area behind the goal was developed, presumably only that which the finances at the time allowed.

The local press reported that: *"The management realises that the weather, although having little effect on the real football fan, where support is concerned, is objected to by many others when the weather is inclined to be wet..... The Griffin Park ground will now be noted for the fact that it has more covered accommodation than the majority of other clubs. The cost of the scheme runs into*

Below: Brentford players train amongst the backdrop of a soon-to-be enlarged New Road terrace.

The Brook Road terrace was extended in the sumer of 1935 to provide one more stage towards completing the ten year plan.

some thousands of pounds, and will, of course, provide many week's' work for a large number of men." The claimed capacity for the Brook Road end was now estimated to be 8,000.

The following season the team almost took off where they had left off, and throughout the season made a serious challenge for a second successive promotion. Always up with the leading pack, they just lost out from the top pair, with 51 points, trailing second placed Preston North End by a single point. The record attendance at Griffin Park was yet again broken when 25,184 managed to gain entry for the local derby game with Fulham in early March.

Strangely the club's success was not reflected in their F.A. Cup performances, for the two most memorable seasons in their history resulted in exits at the first time of asking. It will come as no surprise to find that the Bees recorded their highest (to that date) average attendance that season of 16,377, the fourth best in the Second Division.

Brentford took the Second Division title by storm a year later, the 1934/35 season. By Boxing Day, with just over half the season completed, the Bees had suffered just two defeats, and were already well on their way to Division One. The older supporters and the new found ones flocked into Griffin Park in vast numbers, with the crowd never falling below 14,000, indeed very often it was around the 20,000 mark. Already Champions (they won the divisional title by a clear six points) the match against Sheffield United was won 3-1 to cap the most successful season in the Club's history. Once again there was a new Brentford record average attendance figure, of 18,062, that had packed onto the terraces and into the stand.

Even before the euphoria and exciting prospect of top flight football that was to come to Brentford, the Board had to consider ways in which the ground could be further enlarged in order to house even bigger attendances. Once again, in the close season, a small army of men went into action to carry out the necessary expansion.

Right: Brentford trainer Bob Kane gets stuck into the Ealing Road terrace, much to the amusement of two Brentford players.

October 1935, and workmen build new terrace steps in the Ealing Road/New Road corner in time for The Bees game against Arsenal.

The lopsided Brook Road end was made more symmetrical, with more terracing added to the lower area, and was also roofed to match the existing. A further fewer hundred places for seated supporters was created in the slightly end wings at each end of the Braemar Road stand. This addition made full use of an otherwise unused area, and although each "overlap" the ends of the pitch, there was a perfectly acceptable view from these vantage points. The final extension was that to the New Road side, the terrace was extended backwards by several terrace steps along this side. This entailed re-roofing again and created additional accommodation for 5,000 spectators. Around this time house numbers 62 and 63 were purchased and then demolished in order to provide access turnstiles and exits to that side of the ground.

After the hive of activity that had taken place during the close season, there was just one major area left to fill. In late October, and in time for the Arsenal game (which attracted a massive 34,000 crowd) the undeveloped corner between New Road and Ealing Road (the "bob-a-nob" end as it was known) was in filled with concrete terracing.

Just about every conceivable part of the Griffin Park site had been exploited, but in fact just one further addition was still made. This took place during the summer of 1937, when an even greater standing area was conceived on the popular New Road side. Until this time the perimeter of the pitch consisted of a ground level fence, however now a few steps lower were excavated to bring the front of the enclosure nearer the pitch but below pitch level. Whilst this may have created space for a few hundred more spectators, which now provided accommodation on this side for an estimated 20,000 in total, it was not popular with many who viewed the action almost at eye level with the pitch, and it also created drainage problems, with rainwater building up at this low level.

It had taken over thirty years to reach this stage, but now Brentford were proud to display one of the best spectator friendly, if not largest, grounds in the country. Ample seated areas along the Braemar Road side, extensive concrete terracing elsewhere, two sides of which were fully covered, an estimated capacity for 40,000, and entrances on all four sides of the ground. The pieces were in now place for a future in the top division.

The 1935/36 season started in a blaze of glory, with many players happy to be associated with this new found "big" club. On Thursday the 5th of September, a 25,047 crowd packed into Griffin Park to see their favourites perform in their first-ever home First Division game. The script went as planned and the Bees celebrated their baptism with a 3-1 victory over Blackburn Rovers. This of course being a midweek early evening game, limited the attendance. Two days later - a Saturday - a crowd of 33,481 was admitted - by far a record, being around 5,000 more than the previous best with thousands locked outside. This time the team came down to earth and lost to Huddersfield Town, despite first taking the lead through the diminutive Dai Hopkins.

Another enormous crowd was present for the next game when Aston Villa were the visitors, and this encounter resulted in another defeat; it looked as if Brentford were going to find it an uphill struggle in top flight football. The Autumn encounter with Arsenal was confidently expected to produced yet another record attendance, with 40,000 being expected, but scare stories suggesting of the disasters that might befall spectators in a possible crush, reduced the numbers by several thousands. After a poor start with only two victories in the first eight games, the team took a long time to turn the results in their favour. But they eventually managed to find their feet, and an excellent run-in at the end of the season, which produced a twelve match unbeaten sequence from early March, saw the team finish in a highly creditable fifth place, after at one time being serious contenders for the runners-up spot.

Chelsea were the visitors at the end of March when the new record Griffin Park attendance rose to 33,486. With attendances normally in the high twenty and often thirty thousands, the average at Griffin Park rocketed for this season, to reach 25,287.

On the 25th of March 1936, agreement was finally made with Fullers to purchase Griffin Park. The original lease had expired in 1925 but with the Club more solvent than ever, they could now call the ground well and truly their own.

After their barnstorming run at the end, they were tipped as one of the favourites for the Championship in 1936/37. A more than moderate start was made, with the crowds continuing to flood into the ground, and after defeating Manchester United 4-0 at home the Bees actually led the table for one memorable week. This run of form couldn't quite be sustained, but overall a good record was maintained until March. There was even an outside chance of the Championship, and a fair possibility of the runners-up spot, but in contrast to a year earlier the final run-in to the season was poor. In the last eight games, just two victories were achieved, and a final sixth place in the First Division had to suffice; but it was hardly a poor season.

One of the most satisfying victories was a 5-0 thrashing of the once mighty Huddersfield Town, and fellow First Division

Right: The entrance to the ground on the New Road side. This provided entrances and exits to all four sides of the ground, but was not installed until 1936 when house numbers 62 and 63 were purchased and demolished.

bedfellows, in the F.A.Cup. The Bees had been made second favourites, at 6-1, to win the trophy, but any sustained run in this competition soon ended in the next round at Derby County. Once again the average attendance at Griffin Park remained at a high level for League matches, this time at 24,544, the eighth best in the country.

If the two previous seasons were considered good, then the 1937/38 was little short of amazing - at least for a long period. With some big money signings to bolster the team, the matches started in only a mediocre fashion, before a run of four successive victories took the Bees to the top in mid-October. For Sunderland's visit early that month, a new record attendance was reached at 35,584. Brentford leading the First Division for three months was the undreamed of reality, and after completing the double over reigning Champions Manchester City on the 27th December, it really looked as if the Championship was within their grasp.

But the team slipped badly in February and March, and apart from a spirited revival at the end, including an amazing double over Champions-elect Arsenal, the club finally finished sixth from top. To offset the disappointing League form in the New Year, the team went on the rampage in the F.A. Cup to reach the quarter-finals for the first time. A run of home draws took them through to the last eight, but further progress was terminated at home to Preston North End, with a shock 3-0 defeat.

But the Cup as usual excited the imagination, and after 36,718 packed into the ground for the Portsmouth clash, a few weeks later this record was increased to 37,586 for Preston's visit.

Unbeknown at the time, but the 1938/39 season was to become not only the last full Football League season before a long enforced break due to World War Two, but also the last for Brentford F.C. as a successful member of the First Division. The previous season had without doubt been the most exciting and most successful in the club's 34 years life at Griffin Park, and much was now expected for the forthcoming campaign.

Unfortunately as the season unfolded it became obvious that the best was behind them. A good start - two victories in three games - was followed with a poor run which more or less lasted the rest of the season. The one bright period was an excellent run in February and early March that produced five consecutive victories and then a draw. But far from looking towards the Championship, this sequence did much to raise the club above the relegation zone. With little to play for the season fizzled out, and the crowds not unnaturally dropped, the last two home games attracting just sixteen and twenty-two thousand. In contrast, back in early September 1938, the visit of Arsenal produced yet another new record, of 38,535.

Fifth from bottom of the First Division was the final disappointing outcome; just four points clear of relegation. But with war clouds looming, the 1939/40 season got underway in depressing mood. Brentford, as did other clubs, played just three Football League matches that season before the competition was abandoned. The victory, the last of the trio, on the 2nd of September saw Huddersfield Town beaten 1-0, and the attendance was a below-average 13,000. There was to be an enforced break of seven years before Football League matches were to return to Griffin Park. Physically, everything that could reasonably have been developed at the ground had been accomplished, but the post-war years ahead were to signal periods of floodlights, fire and falling attendances.

Left: Brentford's F.A. Cup Sixth Round tie with Preston North End attractted a crowd of 37,586 to Griffin Park, with "packers" deployed to ensure eveyone got a view of the action.

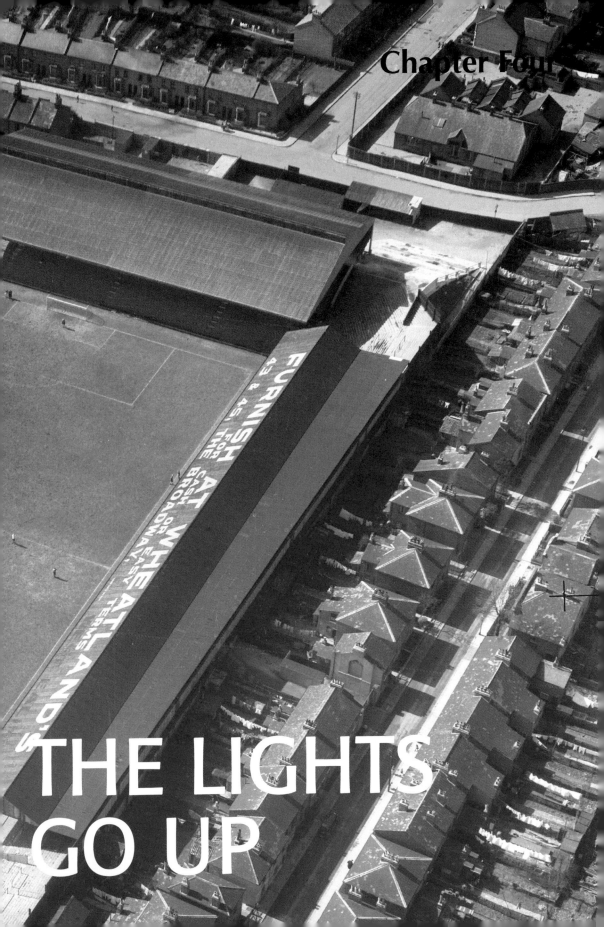

Chapter Four

THE LIGHTS GO UP

Nine years had passed since the end of the Second World War without a change to Griffin Park. It survived bomb damage, unlike fellow London clubs West Ham, Arsenal or Millwall, and remained untouched until floodlit football came along.

Brentford were amongst the first clubs to see the revenue potential in floodlit football, so in 1954, sixty-four 1500-watt bulbs were placed on the Braemar and New Road sides of the ground, mounted on steel supports at roof level. The total cost amounted to £5,345, which was more than recouped over the next few years as the Club several clubs to play floodlit friendlies in front of large crowds. Chelsea were the first visitors on the 5th of October 1954 - winning 4-0 in front of a 11,300 crowd. The next month, over 21,000 – almost double that of The Bees Third Division game against Bournemouth and Boscombe - saw Brentford entertain an International Managers XI, the all-star team including no less than Stanley Matthews and Tom Finney.

By 1963, Brentford's floodlights were slipping behind standards set by other clubs. Having just won the Fourth Division Championship that May, efforts were made to give Griffin Park a much-needed face-lift. During the summer, at a cost of £15,000, four pylons were erected at each corner of the ground to replace the original set. Manager Malcolm MacDonald wryly commented: *"Under the old lights it was very easy to see mistakes, but goodness knows what it will be like under the new ones."*

The steelwork from the old lights, removed from the New Road side in the early 1970s, were still evident on the Braemar Road roof until 1987 when it was taken down to make way for the new parapet sheeting. Brentford christened

Right: An aerial view of Brentford pictured in July 1957. The Wheatland's furniture store advert had by now disappeared from the New Road roof.

Below: Four floodlight plyons were installed in the summer of 1963, each holding 64 lamps.

The Braemar Road frontage gets a much-needed face-lift in 1963.

the new lights with a pre-season friendly against local rivals Queens Park Rangers on August 13th. George Sands from the *Middlesex Chronicle* described a "roar from the crowd" when the 144 bulbs were lit for the first time. The Braemar Road frontage also received a make-over, with a new set of staircases for B and C Blocks, administrative offices built plus new entrances to the bar at ground level. The project was completed in time for The Bees' opening League fixture against Notts County. New turnstile blocks were also built, as Chairman Jack Dunnett matched the cash input off the pitch as he had done on it. However, these were the last major improvements Brentford would make to Griffin Park for twenty years.

Brentford's future at Griffin Park was under the spotlight in 1968, when the board considered an offer from Queens Park Rangers Chairman Jim Gregory to buy Griffin Park for £250,000 Brentford would then use Hillingdon Borough's ground as a permanent base. This offer looked increasingly attractive given the £135,000 debt. Former Brentford Director Walter Wheatley stepped in to offer the club a £69,000 loan, a move that ensured not only Brentford's tenure at Griffin Park but also the Club's survival.

Mr Wheatley eventually became Chairman but was removed in 1974. The new incumbent, Les Davey expressed a desire to

see Brentford move into a new stadium. He pronounced that: *"I know football fans have a traditional affection for tatty old football grounds – but I believe this has become a thing of the past."*

One of the potential sites was the Brentford Market site, now coming to the end of its natural life. This wish was not forthcoming however and Brentford concentrated on Griffin Park. The steelwork holding the first set of floodlights was removed from the New Road roof during the 1973-74 season and the decision was taken to paint red and white stripes along the length of its span, adding a welcome splash of colour to the ground.

In October 1979, Hounslow Council turned down the Club's £200,000 Sports Hall project, situated behind the Brook Road goal, but the local authority indicated that they would assist in finding an alternative site. Undeterred, the board forged ahead three months later with plans to re-build the New Road stand complete with 5,250 seats and 2,250 terrace spaces.

As a sign of the times, the Ealing Road was given over exclusively to visiting supporters as potential for crowd trouble at the ground had necessitated their segregation. Gone were the days when both sets of supporters could swap ends to cheer on their team. On March 31st 1981, a revised application for the New Road stand was finally made to Hounslow Council after consultation with local residents. In September 1981, Martin Lange was appointed Chairman in succession to Dan Tana.

One of his first tasks was to pour cold water on any fresh development of the New Road side of the ground. *"There is no foreseeable prospect in the New Road stand being built. In fact the Board have abandoned this project, other than possibly establishing the planning consent. It is my considered view that firstly, in no way can the Club afford a new stand, and secondly, I am not convinced in any shape or form it would add additional income to the Club."*

The marketing department of the Club pulled off a coup in the summer of 1982 when Dutch Airline K.L.M. agreed to advertise on the New Road stand. This feat was chronicled in the *Guinness Book of Records* as the largest advertisement in Europe. It was the first time an advert had been placed on the roof since Ealing based furniture store Wheatland's did so in the late 1930s.

Owing to the growing trend in spectator unrest, the decision was made in early 1983 to construct a tall segregation fence on the New Road terrace, about twenty yards from the Ealing Road goal line. This gave visiting supporters the choice to stand under cover if the weather was inclement. This wasn't the only change to Griffin Park at this time, and very unexpected it was too.

Shall we strike? A crowd of 15,000 airport workers gathered at Griffin Park on March, 16th 1970 on whether or not to take industrial action.

Chapter Five

THE GREAT FIRE OF BRENTFORD

Griffin Park had remained relatively untouched for nearly fifty years until the late hours of 1st February 1983. A local resident raised the alarm when he spotted flames billowing out of the Braemar Road stand. Soon this would rip through blocks E and F, destroying over 800 plastic "bucket" seats, all of which had been newly installed the summer before. By midnight, a huge orange glow could be seen from miles around the Stadium.

The damage extended beyond the seated areas to beneath the stand as the away dressing room, a gymnasium, kit store and laundry room were all put beyond use. Sixteen strips of playing gear, along with all of the Club's equipment used by physiotherapist Eddie Lyons also perished. Griffin Park's press box, including the recently refurbished press room, were also destroyed. Jane Bowles, wife of midfielder Stan, who both lived in Braemar Road, averted the loss of life by waking Alec Banks, a member of the groundstaff who was sleeping in a hut adjacent to the stand. She told the *Middlesex Chronicle*: "I thought Alec might be there so I just screamed out to him. It was very frightening. I thought for a while our house might be burnt down."

Local residents were directed to the Griffin and Princess Royal

Below: The charred remains of the Braemar Road tunnel.

Soccer club hit by midnight blaze

By Sean Gilligan and Margaret Lyons
Photo: George Harrison

Chronicle backs appeal by fans

Above: The 4th of February edition of The Middlesex Chronicle.

Below: The aftermath of the fire.

public houses to shelter whilst fire fighters from Chiswick, Heston and Acton fought for over two hours to bring the blaze under control. By the next morning, Nottingham Forest, QPR and Watford were amongst the clubs offering to help. Amazingly, electricians worked throughout the day to ensure the Club could stage a reserve team fixture against Northampton Town on the Wednesday evening at Griffin Park. In front of the their biggest crowd of the season, Brentford reserves won 5-3. The Brentford Supporters Association launched a South Stand Appeal Fund in order to raise the estimated £150,000 needed to rebuild the stand, a figure that grew considerably higher after the final audit. The fire was not treated as suspicious, with the possible cause an electrical fault. The two blocks remained closed for the rest of the season, but the paddock below was made accessible to supporters.

Upon the season's close, work commenced on its replacement. Chairman Martin Lange decided this was an opportune time to expand the Club's ability to benefit from the growth in commercial

Players were forced to change at the Ealing Road end in the wake of the fire.

Above: Constructors start work on the new Braemar Road stand.

activity within football. The original 1927 structure was demolished from C Block onwards to make way for a replacement costing £1.2 million with new lounge and gym facilities. The section, designed by local architects J.P. Jelly Partnership, included a new disabled block; the roof held by three supports instead of the previous five. The new structure took four months to complete and fully opened in time for Brentford's Milk Cup tie with Liverpool in October.

In June 1983, the club announced a new £150,000 Sports Hall, partly funded by the Sports Council and situated behind the Brook Road Stand. Similar to the project mooted four years earlier, the new hall would cater for Badminton, Basketball and a five-a-side pitch. A jacuzzi, sauna, sun-beds and a gym area for aerobatics were also envisaged. These plans were ultimately shelved, presumably due to lack of funds. Just around the corner was a tradegy that would change Griffin Park for good.

Chapter Six

DEATH OF THE
ROYAL OAK

Saturday, 11th May 1985 was to signal the beginning of the end of the traditional football ground. On that day, fifty-six people died after a discarded cigarette caused a fire at Bradford's last home match of the season, which spread to the entire main stand. Exit gates were locked and a lack of fire extinguishers compounded efforts to quell the blaze.

Legislation to govern sports stadia was weak, with The Safety of Sports Grounds Act drafted in 1975 in response to the tragedy at Ibrox four years earlier when sixty-six people were killed on the notorious Stairway 13. It introduced a system of compulsory licensing, but only for the top two divisions in England. Following the events at Valley Parade, a preliminary enquiry set up to look into the fire extended this rule to include all stadiums with a capacity above 10,000 – the change effective 9th of August 1985, in time for the new Canon League season.

As a result of this, Griffin Park was destined to change forever. Work on Griffin Park just to bring it up to scratch for the new season meant a significant outlay to keep the four sides of the ground open, estimated at £160,000. Griffin Park's total capacity was slashed from 37,000 to 10,600. Tests were carried out on

Below: Twelve flats under construction tower over the Ealing Road terrace for Brentford's League match with Wolverhampton Wanderers in August 1985.

the Ealing Road crush barriers and these required strengthening, as did the perimeter fence. A, B, C and Y blocks of Braemar Road were of wooden construction, making their renovation hugely expensive. A Block was not considered cost-effective to renovate and was closed. Emergency lighting required by the new legislation meant just the Braemar Road stand being opened for The Bees Milk Cup tie with Cambridge United that month.

Brentford Chairman Martin Lange had overseen the construction of the new Braemar Road stand throughout 1983. This complied with all the regulations of the Act's "Green Code" so minimal expenditure was required. His biggest concern however, was the Brook Road end and New Road terrace. Sections of both stands had been fenced off in recent years due to disrepair. Mr Lange decided that the cost of maintaining both areas in their present form was not viable.

Planning permission was granted in March 1985 to build twelve flats - christened "Bowles Hall" after ex-Bees midfielder Stanley - in the open area behind the Ealing Road terrace. Work started straight away but the delay in alterations to the entrance in Ealing Road had caused the postponement of a League fixture against Millwall on March 16th, as the G.L.C decided that visiting supporters could not be segregated effectively. Finished in autumn 1985, the very top floor apartments enjoy, as they do today, an excellent view of the pitch.

To ease the burden of the Club's debt even further, a planning application was made to Hounslow Council during the summer

for the construction of thirty flats behind the Brook Road end. The sale of land to developers would help to clear the estimated two thousand pound a week losses currently being incurred.

This development was initially refused but later upheld on appeal. Perhaps mindful of Griffin Park being newly designated, the Club made a revised application. This time a larger residential complex of 48 flats was envisaged, with the demolition of the beloved "Royal Oak" End. The Brentford Chairman gave his reasons behind the scheme in the matchday programme against Derby County in November 1985, commenting that the changes: *"will certainly provide the means to completely repay our bank overdraft, and thereby remove the interest payment element from our current overheads. In addition it should also go a long way towards paying Directors' loans. I have stated in the past that the Club must ultimately achieve a situation where it stands on its own two feet and ways its way, as with any other business undertaking. Failure to do so will result in the Club's demise."*

Many lamented the loss of Griffin Park's "kop" at the time, but given the Club's financial state, accepted its fate. Therefore, it must have been galling for those supporters to see the Club's debt stand at £1.5 million six years later.

The Royal Oak was used for the last time on the 15th January 1986 in a low-key Freight Rover Trophy tie against a Derby County team who fielded seven reserves - an ignominious end to a terrace that has now passed into Brentford folklore. Towards the

Below: Summer 1986, and wooden terracing is removed from the back of the New Road stand.

end of that season, nothing more than rubble could be witnessed from behind the goal, the lack of atmosphere perhaps a factor in Brentford winning only one more home game that season, albeit the last of the campaign against Darlington (a match that attracted Griffin Park's lowest attendance for nearly fifty years).

Rather than creating a new standing section, it was decided to save the bottom thirteen rows of terracing from the Oak to form the new stand's base – a presumably cheaper option. Over the summer, the new stand and accompanying flats behind began to rise. The design of the new stand came in for criticism in some quarters - nicknamed "The Wendy House" by some - but others heralded Brentford's forward thinking. What cannot be disputed

Left: August 1986 and the Brook Road takes shape as Robbie Cooke scores from the penalty spot against AFC Bournemouth.

is the new structure put paid to the west wing of the Braemar Road stand being used again for spectators, as most of the 400 seats in that area could now not see the Brook Road goal – a terrible waste. The northwest terrace corner of Griffin Park was also demolished, making way for a car park.

The condemned terracing to the rear of the New Road was removed and parapet sheeting installed to form a backing, effectively cutting the stand's size in half. The steelwork behind was left untouched, with the initial intention to open this again if the team were attracting high enough attendances to warrant it.

The official opening of the now christened "family stand" was against Middlesbrough in December 1986. The two-tier structure accommodated 636 seats on the top tier with 3000 terrace places below. The view from the top tier is arguably the finest from Griffin Park, giving an unobstructed view of the pitch. In the close season of 1987, it was time for the old section of the Braemar Road stand to receive a face-lift. The roof above A, B and C Block was replaced and the paddock wall beneath it re-built. The terracing, now a "members only" section on matchdays, was left untouched. Grey parapet sheeting was installed at the bottom of the roof, and gave the stand a feeling of symmetry with its new neighbour. It was four years before any further work of significance was undertaken.

Below: 48 flats on the Brook Road take shape after the demolition of the Royal Oak. Finished ahead of schedule, these flats cleared the Club's ever-increasing overdraft, albeit temporarily.

TAYLOR AND
BEYOND

Chapter Seven

The Hillsborough Disaster in 1989, in which ninety-six Liverpool fans lost their lives, caused a huge change to sports stadia across the county. The Taylor report, which examined the tradegy, ordered the top two divisions to turn their grounds into all-seater stadiums by 1994, and the bottom two by 1999, although the latter was rescinded. A select group of First Division Club Chairman decided that the Football League did not offer them enough revenue to carry out these improvements. The F.A. Premier League was subsequently formed, enabling the top Division to siphon off a bigger chunk of the ever-increasing television revenue.

High perimeter fences were pulled down all over the country in the wake of Hillsborough, but as these were never installed at Griffin Park, minimal action such as highlighting entrance exit gates in a different colour to the perimeter fence was needed

However, the Ealing Road terrace had come to the end of its lifespan, its capacity gradually reduced from 6000 in 1984 to a mere 793 in 1990-91. Before the next season started, Hounslow Council condemned its use. Visiting supporters who wished to stand were housed exclusively in the New Road "away" pen before construction started on re-profiling the terrace. Once this commenced, access to that part of the ground was no longer possible, with all visiting supporters placed in B Block.

As part of the work, the Ealing Road turnstiles were demolished to provide an exit only. Due to new regulations on entrance and exit widths, installing new turnstile blocks would lower the licensed capacity. In this new age of safety, it was a question

Right: Supporters clear the pitch to ensure Brentford's League fixture with Exeter City in February 1991 goes ahead.

Above: February 1992, and Dean Holdsworth scores against Stockport County in front of an Ealing Road terrace undergoing complete refurbishment.

of how many people could be evacuated within a certain time limit, rather than squeezing fans onto a square yard of terrace. All future admittance to the Ealing Road terrace would be therefore made via the Braemar Road side of the ground.

Not only would Ealing Road be upgraded, the east wing of Braemar Road – A Block, which had lain unused since the mid 1980s, be refurbished. Both projects were assisted by grant aid. Increasing the ground's capacity was a welcome bonus as on the pitch, Brentford were enjoying their most successful seasons in recent memory. A Block was completed in March 1992, in time for The Bees' home game against AFC Bournemouth. This increased the ground's capacity by a further 650 seats.

The Ealing Road terrace was finally re-opened in time for Brentford's April derby with Fulham – minus crush barriers. Because of this, a safety limit of just over a thousand for the terrace was set (Fulham fans were given the Brook Road end for this fixture). Supporters that stood on the open end in the pouring rain no doubt enjoyed one of Griffin Park's most memorable games as 12,071 people watched Brentford rout their near neighbours 4-0.

Promotion, and the Championship, was secured with a 1-0 victory at Peterborough United, Brentford looked forward to playing in their highest level of football in 38 years with a new capacity of just under 14,000 - the highest for some years. Over the summer, further work was undertaken. CCTV was installed on all four roads surrounding the ground, with a new police control box placed adjacent to the Brook Road stand. Crush barriers were finally installed on the Ealing Road terrace. The tall dividing fence in New Road was taken down after ten years, as the decision was made to accommodate away supporters exclusively in the Brook Road stand, in view of the anticipated rise in visiting support.

After such optimism, The Bees spent just a single season in Division One, being relegated in May 1993 on the final day of the campaign. One small change that took place during the summer summer was the demolition of the original New Road turnstile blocks built in 1936. The turnstiles were removed, refurbished and then re-positioned with new lighting and boundary wall. This was completed in time for the start of the 1993-94 season.

In September 1993, plans were released to re-build the New Road and Ealing Road stands. This was the first phase of a project to increase the ground's capacity to 15,000. The New Road roof

Below: Construction Company Norwest Holst's vision of a post-Taylor Griffin Park was unveiled in September 1993.

Right: Prawn sandwiches anyone? 1993 plans for executive boxes on the New Road side were eventually shelved.

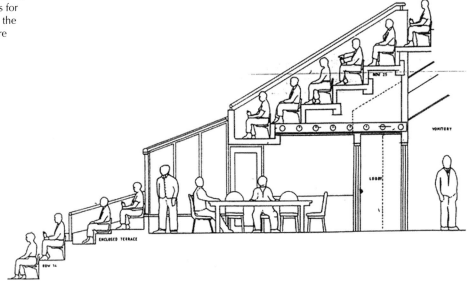

SECTION THROUGH HOSPITALITY UNIT

would be replaced with a cantilever structure and executive boxes installed at the back, the Ealing Road given a roof for the first time. In view of the club's financial predicament, this was a surprise. It took until October 1994 before Brentford submitted a planning application, but a smaller project entailed; this time for a roof on the Ealing Road terrace. Local residents were far from impressed with the plans. The decision was made to reject the application, with Brentford's appeal to the Secretary of State failing in 1995. It would take another ten years before the club made an attempt to try again.

Saturday, the 4th of May 1996 was to be the last time the New Road and Braemar Road paddock were used as a terrace after 92 years of service. After that 2-0 win over AFC Bournemouth, both stands received grant-aid money to be turned into seated accommodation. The Braemar Road paddock was completed in time for Brentford's first league match against Luton Town in August 1996, but the New Road was partially finished, as only one block of seats were made available to Season Ticket holders only. This work was finished by September - the last major alteration to the ground thus far.

In June 1998, Ron Noades took control of Brentford Football Club and made no disguise of his desire to move away from Griffin Park. Hounslow Council included in their election manifesto the desire to build a new stadium, and Brentford would be a prominent partner. The site chosen was land adjacent to the Western International Market site in Hayes, right on the Borough's northwest border.

Former Chairman Martin Lange, who still owned a sizeable

proportion of the Club's shares, backed the plan alongside Cllr Chatt, Leader of Hounslow Council. The project's conception was dogged by obstacles and eventually abandoned, with both sides seemingly apportioning blame on the other. In 2001, the Club switched the away support back to the Ealing Road, giving visitors an increased allocation and Brentford fans a covered home end that they craved for. The policy seemed to work as The Bees narrowly missed out on promotion with a superb home record.

On October 13th 2001, footballing history was made at Griffin Park. Never before had a League match been staged with no admission charge. Other clubs had opened their doors to their own fans, but this was the first time the offer had been made to the visiting team. 11,097 spectators - including nearly 3,000 from Peterborough, enoyed an afternoon of football without spending a penny. On a hot day, Brentford ran out 3-2 winners in an exciting contest.

Around the same time Brentford announced Rugby League side London Broncos would groundshare in time for the new 2002 Super League season. Griffin Park had already hosted two

Joe Omigie evades the attention of Queens Park Rangers defender Alan McDonald in a Jul;y 1996 pre-season friendly between the two teams. Note the work to turn the New Road into a seated stand.

Summer 1996, and the Braemar Road paddock is re-profiled and seated.

televised London Broncos fixtures with great success in 1995.

In November 2002, the Brentford Supporters' Trust - Bees United – announced plans for a new stadium in Lionel Road, one mile to the east of Griffin Park. The 18,000 capacity all-seater venue would also be the centre of a transport hub to serve the local community. In February 2004, the Club appeared to adopt a twin-track approach, submitting plans to Hounslow Council to improve Griffin Park's facilities in tandem with the quest for a new home.

The New Road stand would have function rooms and toilets installed at the back, with both wings of the Braemar Road stand demolished to make way for refreshment and toilets. The Ealing Road would be roofed for the first time and the Brook Road terrace extended to beneath ground level to provide extra capacity.

Griffin Park has also become a seat of learning. During the winter of 2003, the "Bees Inn" bar situated in D Block was refurbished and transformed into the Griffin Park Learning Zone

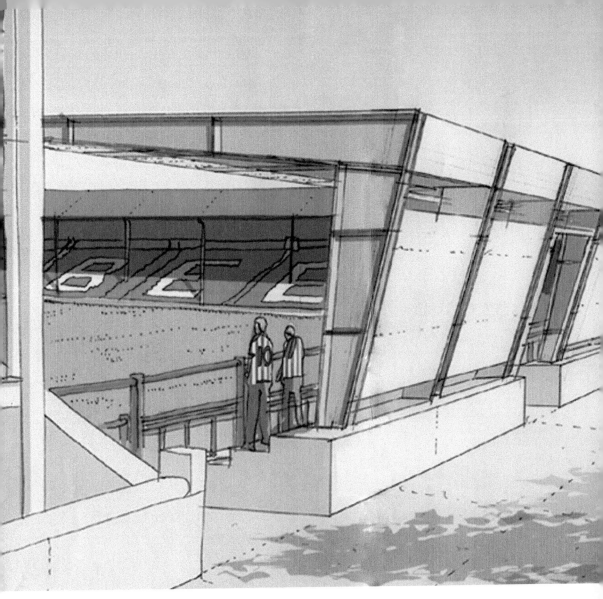

Above: An artist's impression of the proposed Ealing Road roof as part of plans submitted to Hounslow Council in 2004.

under the Government initiative "Playing for Success". Launched in March 2004, children of all ages attend classes on a daily basis that are themed on football.

At the time of writing, it is not known whether the latest plans to improve Griffin Park are successful but one thing is for certain, the story still continues. It is doubtful that Griffin Park will be around for another 100 years, but its presence has provided hours of enjoyment for many thousands of Brentford fans of all ages.

Left: 1998 plans for the "Bee Dome" are unveiled at Griffin Park.

Griffin Park Centenary Day

Sunday 25th July 2004 will long be etched in the minds and hearts of players and supporters alike. Nearly a hundred ex-Brentford players made the trip back to help the Club celebrate Griffin Park's Centenary.

Reading were chosen as opponents, made all the more special with the inclusion of five ex-Bees (Ivar Ingimarsson, Ibrahima Sonko, Steven Sidwell, Nicky Forster and Lloyd Owusu) in their starting line-up. Brentford wore a replica of the kit worn in the 1904-05 season.

After the main match, which Brentford won 1-0, an ex-Bees exhibition match took place after the main match .Prior to the game, the two teams were presented to the "Guest of Honour" Bill Axbey, who celebrated his own Centenary, months earlier.

The Blue and Yellows secured a 3-2 victory against the Red and Whites. Their scorers were Dean Holdsworth, Billy Manuel and the Player/Manager, whilst Barry Silkman and Sean Sparham replied for the Red and Whites.

The Brentford "Walk of Fame" took place during at half time during the main match. Each player was introduced individually and then made "the walk" to the centre circle where a group photo was taken to record the special moment.

The players who took part in the "Walk" were:

John Fielding, Gerry Cakebread, George Lowden, Wally Bragg, Les Devonshire, Fred Durrant, Ken Horne, Paul Priddy, George Dobson, Bill Slater, Tom Anthony, Denny Mundee, Brian Statham, Bob Booker, Terry

Evans, Marcus Gayle, Keith Millen, Robbie Carroll, Allan Cockram, Graham Benstead, Billy Manuel, Dean Holdsworth, Danis Salman, Andy Driscoll, Sean Sparham, Gary Roberts, Glenn Cockerill, Jim McNichol, Brian Tawse, Pat Kruse, Barry Silkman, Terry Rowe, Bobby Ross, Johnny Brooks, Mickey Ball, Willie Graham, Graham Pearce, Jackie Graham, Dougie Allder, Paul Bence, Andy Woon, Terry Scales, Gordon Phillips, Gordon Sweetzer, Mark Hill, Dennis Heath, Alan Hawley, Gary Towse, Eddie Reeve, Nigel Smith, Andy Scott, Gavin Mahon, Jason Pearcey, Robert Quinn, Darren Powell, Danny Boxall, Paul Gibbs and Ted Gaskell.

Internationals at Griffin Park

War-time International – 18th April 1942.
Holland 2 France 0
Attendance: 20,000.

War-time International - 12th December 1942.
Holland 0 Belgium 0

Schoolboy International – 8th May 1948.
England 0 Republic of Ireland 1
Attendance: 14,000.

1948 Olympics – 2nd August 1948.
Italy 9 U.S.A. 0
Attendance: 8,000.

Youth International – 2nd March 1957.
England 5 Holland 5

U.E.F.A. Youth Tournament – 13th April 1963.
U.S.S.R 0 Romania 1
Attendance: 2,500.

Amateur International - 11th March 1966.
England 4 Republic of Ireland 0

Schoolboy Friendly – 30th March 1988.
England 1 Brazil 0
Attendance: 12,000.

UEFA European Championship for Women – 1st October 1989.
England 0 Finland 0

UEFA Under-21 Championship - 26th March 1991.
England 3 Republic of Ireland 0
Attendance: 9,120.

Under-21 International Friendly – 8th March 1994.
England 1 Denmark 0
Attendance: 11,553.

UEFA European Championship for Women – 17th April 1994.
England 10 Slovenia 0

UEFA European Championship for Women – 19th May 1996.
England 3 Portugal 0

Griffin Park Facts and Figures

Highest Attendance: 38,678 v Leicester City, F.A. Cup Sixth Round, 26th February 1949.

Highest League Attendance: 38,535 v Arsenal, 8th September 1938.

Lowest League Attendance: 2,202 v Walsall, 5th December 1927.

Lowest FA Cup Attendance: 1,475 v First Battalion King's Royal Rifles, Nov 18 1911, Fourth Qualifying Round, (drew 1-1).

Lowest League Cup Attendance: 2,040 v Shrewsbury Town, Coca-Cola Cup First Round, 1997.

Lowest Official Griffin Park attendance for a competitive game: 1,100 v Swindon Town, 6 January 1987, Freight Rover Trophy, First Round, (won 4-2).

Highest Average Attendance: 25,768, 1946-47 season.

Lowest Average Attendance: 3,918, 1986-87 season.

First Griffin Park Friendly: 26th September 1904 v Wellingborough (won 3-0).

First Griffin Park Floodlit Match: 5th October 1954 v Chelsea (lost 4-0).

First Griffin Park League Game: 30th August 1920 v Millwall (won 1-0).

First Griffin Park F.A. Cup Game: 14th January 1905 v Reading (drew 1-1).

First Griffin Park League Cup Game: 25th October 1960 v Sunderland (won 4-3).

Griffin Park Attendances 1925-2004

The following list provides Brentford's season by season attendance information since 1925 when the Football League began collating accurate information.

Season	League	Average Att.	Highest	Lowest
1925-1926	Division Three (S)	9146	16893 v Millwall	5632 v Aberdare Atheltic
1926-1927	Division Three (S)	9713	17380 v Queens Park Rangers	4775 v Northampton
1927-1928	Division Three (S)	7331	12513 v Millwall	2202 v Walsall
1928-1929	Division Three (S)	8159	20783 v Queens Park Rangers	4507 v Torquay United
1929-1930	Division Three (S)	12123	21966 v Fulham	6265 v Bristol Rovers
1930-1931	Division Three (S)	8236	11356 v Northampton Town	4327 v Swindon Town
1931-1932	Division Three (S)	11347	26139 v Fulham	4902 v Mansfield Town
1932-1933	Division Three (S)	13300	20693 v Norwich City	8377 v Coventry City
1933-1934	Division Two	16377	26934 v Grimsby Town	12017 v Millwall
1934-1935	Division Two	18062	26079 v Newcastle United	11843 v Barnsley
1935-1936	Division One	25287	33486 v Chelsea	15379 v Portsmouth
1936-1937	Division One	24544	31745 v Derby County	14103 v Grimsby Town
1937-1938	Division One	23335	35584 v Sunderland	14609 v Birmingham
1938-1939	Division One	23117	38535 v Arsenal	12761 v Blackpool
1946-1947	Division One	25768	35604 v Wolverhampton W.	17976 v Arsenal
1947-1948	Division Two	23341	34483 v Cardiff City	13723 v Plymouth Argyle
1948-1949	Division Two	22755	31360 v West Ham United	14360 v Plymouth Argyle
1949-1950	Division Two	22613	33791 v Hull City	16384 v Grimsby Town
1950-1951	Division Two	19593	26393 v Notts County	9808 v Luton Town
1951-1952	Division Two	23022	35827 v Sheffield Wednesday	10243 v Doncaster Rovers
1952-1953	Division Two	17474	29241 v Fulham	8565 v Birmingham City
1953-1954	Division Two	15626	22845 v Leicester City	10652 v Derby County
1954-1955	Division Three (S)	11077	18756 v Queens Park Rangers	4960 v Newport County
1955-1956	Division Three (S)	10302	17847 v Leyton Orient	4291 v Newport County
1956-1957	Division Three (S)	11482	18760 v Watford	6088 v Millwall
1957-1958	Division Three (S)	13084	25744 v Brighton & Hove A.	9130 v Walsall
1958-1959	Division Three	13924	28725 v Plymouth Argyle	9432 v Rochdale
1959-1960	Division Three	11912	21634 v Norwich City	6328 v Chesterfield
1960-1961	Division Three	7392	16673 v Watford	3503 v Port Vale
1961-1962	Division Three	8483	18127 v Grimsby Town	3583 v Hull City
1962-1963	Division Four	11418	15820 v Crewe Alexandra	8340 v Mansfield Town
1963-1964	Division Three	11883	16843 v Bristol City	6818 v Hull City
1964-1965	Division Three	10740	16065 v Bristol City	6164 v Scunthorpe United
1965-1966	Division Three	8416	15209 v Queens Park Rangers	4457 v Gillingham
1966-1967	Division Four	6663	10646 v Southend United	3592 v Port Vale
1967-1968	Division Four	6211	9481 v Aldershot	3749 v Workington
1968-1969	Division Four	6419	9806 v Aldershot	3361 v Notts County
1969-1970	Division Four	7773	12261 v Aldershot	4383 v Newport County
1970-1971	Division Four	6776	10058 v Northampton Town	4176 v Peterborough United
1971-1972	Division Four	11738	18521 v Chester City	8712 v Hartlepool United
1972-1973	Division Three	8742	11803 v Bolton Wanderers	6067 v Wrexham
1973-1974	Division Four	5063	8717 v Reading	3166 v Darlington
1974-1975	Division Four	5172	6485 v Reading	3983 v Workington
1975-1976	Division Four	5096	10612 v Reading	3453 v Bradford City
1976-1977	Division Four	5121	8951 v Southend United	3158 v Workington
1977-1978	Division Four	8578	14496 v Watford	5492 v Northampton Town

1978-1979	Division Three	7455	13873 v Watford	5140 v Walsall
1979-1980	Division Three	7818	13674 v Sheffield United	4992 v Rotherham United
1980-1981	Division Three	6752	11610 v Fulham	4883 v Chesterfield
1981-1982	Division Three	5693	10834 v Fulham	4124 v Doncaster Rovers
1982-1983	Division Three	6184	12593 v Portsmouth	4413 v Doncaster Rovers
1983-1984	Division Three	4735	8042 v Burnley	3391 v Rotherham United
1984-1985	Division Three	4074	5254 v Bristol Rovers	3021 v Walsall
1985-1986	Division Three	3957	6351 v Reading	2824 v Darlington
1986-1987	Division Three	3918	7443 v Swindon Town	3057 v Notts County
1987-1988	Division Three	4581	8712 v Fulham	3122 v Doncaster Rovers
1988-1989	Division Three	5682	10851 v Fulham	4013 v Notts County
1989-1990	Division Three	5662	7962 v Fulham	4537 v Bolton Wanderers
1990-1991	Division Three	6144	8021 v Southend United	4812 v Chester City
1991-1992	Division Three	7156	12071 v Fulham	4586 v Hull City
1992-1993	Division One	8476	11912 v West Ham United	6334 v Peterborough United
1993-1994	Division Two	5611	6848 v Reading	4305 v AFC Bournemouth
1994-1995	Division Two	6536	10979 v AFC Bournemouth	4301 v Rotherham United
1995-1996	Division Two	4768	7878 v Swindon Town	3104 v Carlisle United
1996-1997	Division Two	5832	8679 v Watford	3675 v Notts County
1997-1998	Division Two	5029	10510 v Fulham	3424 v Carlisle United
1998-1999	Division Two	5444	9535 v Cardiff City	3674 v Carlisle United
1999-2000	Division Two	5683	7100 v Preston North End	4055 v Wrexham
2000-2001	Division Two	4654	7550 v Reading	3062 v Cambridge United
2001-2002	Division Two	6714	11303 v Reading	4561 v Port Vale
2002-2003	Division Two	5742	9168 v Queens Park Rangers	3990 v Colchester United
2003-2004	Division Two	5542	9485 v AFC Bournemouth	3818 v Blackpool

Griffin Park
Match by Match
1904-2004

A complete listing of Brentford's first-team fixtures
at Griffin Park from 1904 to 2004.

1904-1905

Southern League Division One

Sep 3 1904	West Ham United	D 0-0
Sep 17 1904	Bristol Rovers	L 0-1
Oct 1 1904	Portsmouth	L 1-3
Oct 22 1904	Millwall Athletic	W 2-0
Nov 5 1904	Luton Town	W 3-0
Nov 19 1904	New Brompton	L 0-1
Dec 3 1904	Southampton	L 0-1
Dec 17 1904	Watford	D 1-1
Jan 7 1905	Reading	D 0-0
Jan 21 1905	Northampton Town	L 3-4
Feb 4 1905	Brighton and Hove Albion	W 1-0
Feb 11 1905	Queens Park Rangers	D 0-0
Feb 25 1905	Tottenham Hotspur	D 0-0
Mar 11 1905	Swindon Town	D 1-1
Mar 25 1905	Wellingborough	W 3-0
Apr 8 1905	Fulham	D 1-1
Apr 22 1905	Plymouth Argyle	W 1-0

Western League

Sep 1 1904	Plymouth Argyle	D 1-1
Nov 21 1904	Fulham	W 1-0
Dec 26 1904	Millwall Athletic	W 2-0
Jan 2 1905	West Ham United	W 2-1
Jan 9 1905	Southampton	W 1-0
Feb 27 1905	Reading	W 3-0
Mar 6 1905	Portsmouth	D 0-0
Mar 13 1905	Bristol Rovers	W 3-1
Apr 3 1905	Tottenham Hotspur	W 2-0
Apr 24 1905	Queens Park Rangers	D 1-1

F.A. Cup

| Jan 14 1905 | Reading (Intermediate Round) | D 1-1 |

1905-1906

Southern League Division One

Sep 9 1905	Reading	W 2-1
Sep 23 1905	Brighton and Hove Albion	W 2-0
Oct 7 1905	Fulham	L 0-2
Oct 21 1905	Bristol Rovers	W 1-0
Nov 4 1905	Portsmouth	D 1-1
Nov 18 1905	Millwall Athletic	D 1-1
Dec 2 1905	Tottenham Hotspur	L 0-3
Dec 23 1905	Plymouth Argyle	W 1-0
Dec 30 1905	Southampton	W 2-1
Jan 20 1906	Watford	W 3-0
Feb 17 1906	Queens Park Rangers	D 2-2
Mar 3 1906	New Brompton	W 3-2
Mar 12 1906	Northampton Town	W 2-1
Mar 17 1906	Swindon Town	W 3-1
Mar 31 1906	Luton Town	W 2-1
Apr 21 1906	Norwich City	L 0-2
Apr 23 1906	West Ham United	W 3-1

Western League

Sep 4 1905	Queens Park Rangers	L 1-2
Sep 11 1905	Plymouth Argyle	D 0-0
Oct 2 1905	West Ham United	L 0-2
Oct 9 1905	Southampton	L 1-3
Dec 26 1905	Fulham	W 3-2
Jan 1 1906	Bristol Rovers	W 1-0
Feb 26 1906	Tottenham Hotspur	L 0-1
Mar 19 1906	Portsmouth	L 0-1
Apr 2 1906	Millwall Athletic	W 2-1
Apr 13 1906	Reading	W 3-1

F.A. Cup

Dec 9 1905	Wycombe Wanderers (Fourth Qualifying Round)	W 4-0
Jan 13 1906	Bristol City (First Round)	W 2-1
Feb 3 1906	Lincoln City (Second Round)	W 3-0

1906-1907

Southern League Division One

Sep 1 1906	Watford	W 2-0
Sep 15 1906	Queens Park Rangers	W 4-1
Sep 29 1906	Southampton	W 2-1
Oct 13 1906	Tottenham Hotspur	D 2-2
Oct 27 1906	Norwich City	W 2-1
Nov 10 1906	Crystal Palace	W 2-0
Dec 1 1906	Leyton	W 2-0
Dec 15 1906	New Brompton	W 3-0
Dec 25 1906	Brighton and Hove Albion	W 3-1
Jan 5 1907	Northampton Town	W 2-0
Jan 26 1907	Fulham	W 1-0
Feb 9 1907	West Ham United	D 0-0
Mar 9 1907	Luton Town	L 0-1
Mar 23 1907	Bristol Rovers	W 2-1
Mar 30 1907	Millwall Athletic	L 0-2
Apr 1 1907	Reading	W 4-2
Apr 8 1907	Swindon Town	W 5-2
Apr 13 1907	Portsmouth	D 1-1
Apr 27 1907	Plymouth Argyle	W 2-1

Western League - Section A

Sep 10 1906	Chelsea	W 3-1
Oct 1 1906	Reading	W 4-2
Oct 22 1906	Fulham	W 5-0
Nov 5 1906	Queens Park Rangers	W 2-1
Nov 19 1906	Bristol Rovers	W 2-1

F.A. Cup

Jan 12 1907	Glossop (First Round)	W 2-1
Feb 2 1907	Middlesbrough (Second Round)	W 1-0
Feb 27 1907	Crystal Palace (Third Round replay)	L 0-1

1907-1908

Southern League Division One

Sep 14 1907	Leyton	W 2-0
Sep 28 1907	Watford	W 4-1
Oct 12 1907	Northampton Town	W 3-1
Oct 26 1907	Plymouth Argyle	W 2-1
Nov 9 1907	Queens Park Rangers	D 1-1

Nov 23 1907	Swindon Town	W 2-0
Dec 7 1907	Luton Town	W 3-1
Dec 21 1907	Portsmouth	D 1-1
Dec 25 1907	Millwall Athletic	L 1-2
Jan 4 1908	Bristol Rovers	L 0-3
Jan 18 1908	Reading	W 1-0
Feb 15 1908	Southampton	W 4-0
Feb 29 1908	West Ham United	W 4-0
Mar 9 1908	Norwich City	W 2-1
Mar 14 1908	Tottenham Hotspur	W 3-0
Mar 28 1908	Crystal Palace	D 1-1
Apr 11 1908	Brighton and Hove Albion	W 2-0
Apr 20 1908	New Brompton	W 1-0
Apr 25 1908	Bradford (Park Avenue)	L 1-2

Western League - Section A

Sep 25 1907	Queens Park Rangers	D 1-1
Oct 7 1907	Southampton	D 3-3
Oct 16 1907	Brighton and Hove Albion	W 2-1
Oct 21 1907	Leyton	W 4-0
Oct 28 1907	Portsmouth	L 0-4
Nov 25 1907	Plymouth Argyle	D 0-0

F.A. Cup

Jan 15 1908	Carlisle United (First Round replay)	L 1-3

1908-1909

Southern League Division One

Sep 5 1908	Southampton	L 2-3
Sep 19 1908	West Ham United	W 1-0
Sep 28 1908	Queens Park Rangers	D 0-0
Oct 3 1908	Crystal Palace	L 1-3
Oct 24 1908	Swindon Town	W 1-0
Nov 16 1908	Exeter City	L 0-2
Nov 21 1908	New Brompton	D 1-1
Nov 23 1908	Southend United	W 4-1
Dec 19 1908	Bristol Rovers	D 2-2
Dec 25 1908	Watford	W 3-1
Dec 28 1908	Reading	L 2-3
Jan 9 1909	Leyton	D 0-0
Jan 30 1909	Brighton and Hove Albion	W 4-0
Feb 13 1909	Plymouth Argyle	W 1-0
Feb 20 1909	Luton Town	D 2-2
Mar 20 1909	Northampton Town	W 3-1

Mar 29 1909	Portsmouth	L 1-2
Apr 3 1909	Millwall Athletic	W 4-2
Apr 9 1909	Norwich City	W 3-1
Apr 17 1909	Coventry City	W 5-2

Western League

Sep 7 1908	Plymouth Argyle	L 1-2
Oct 12 1908	West Ham United	L 0-1
Oct 26 1908	Bristol Rovers	W 2-1
Nov 2 1906	Millwall Athletic	L 0-1
Jan 4 1909	Southampton	W 3-0
Jan 25 1909	Portsmouth	W 4-0

United League

Mar 15 1909	Croydon Common	W 2-1
Apr 5 1909	Hastings United	W 2-0
Apr 21 1909	New Brompton	L 1-4
Apr 26 1909	Southend United	D 1-1

F.A. Cup

| Jan 16 1909 | Gainsborough Trinity (First Round) | W 2-0 |

1909-1910

Southern League Division One

Sep 4 1909	Brighton and Hove Albion	D 0-0
Sep 13 1909	Crystal Palace	W 1-0
Sep 18 1909	Portsmouth	W 2-0
Sep 27 1909	Swindon Town	D 1-1
Oct 2 1909	Norwich City	L 0-2
Oct 11 1909	Plymouth Argyle	D 2-2
Oct 23 1909	Watford	W 2-0
Nov 6 1909	Southend United	W 4-1
Dec 18 1909	New Brompton	W 4-1
Dec 25 1909	Northampton Town	W 2-1
Jan 1 1910	Queens Park Rangers	L 0-1
Jan 15 1910	Croydon Common	L 1-2
Jan 22 1910	West Ham United	D 0-0
Feb 14 1910	Bristol Rovers	W 1-0
Feb 19 1910	Exeter City	W 3-0
Feb 26 1910	Coventry City	W 3-1
Mar 12 1910	Reading	W 1-0
Mar 26 1910	Leyton	W 1-0
Mar 28 1910	Luton Town	D 2-2

| Apr 9 1910 | Southampton | W 1-0 |
| Apr 23 1910 | Millwall Athletic | W 2-0 |

F.A. Cup

| Nov 20 1909 | Luton Town (Fourth Qualifying Round) | W 2-1 |

1910-1911

Southern League Division One

Sep 10 1910	Swindon Town	D 1-1
Sep 24 1910	Crystal Palace	W 2-1
Oct 1 1910	Norwich City	W 2-0
Oct 15 1910	Watford	W 2-0
Oct 29 1910	Southampton	W 3-2
Nov 12 1910	Coventry City	W 1-0
Nov 26 1910	Millwall Athletic	W 3-1
Dec 10 1910	West Ham United	W 3-0
Dec 24 1910	Portsmouth	W 2-0
Dec 27 1910	Northampton Town	D 0-0
Dec 31 1910	Exeter City	W 3-1
Jan 21 1911	Bristol Rovers	W 3-0
Feb 11 1911	Leyton	D 0-0
Feb 25 1911	Plymouth Argyle	L 1-2
Mar 11 1911	Southend United	W 3-1
Mar 25 1911	New Brompton	L 0-2
Apr 8 1911	Queens Park Rangers	D 1-1
Apr 17 1911	Brighton and Hove Albion	D 1-1
Apr 22 1911	Luton Town	W 1-0

F.A. Cup

| Jan 14 1911 | Preston North End (First Round) | L 0-1 |

1911-1912

Southern League Division One

Sep 9 1911	Watford	W 4-2
Sep 23 1911	Exeter City	W 3-1
Sep 30 1911	Luton Town	L 0-1
Oct 14 1911	Millwall Athletic	D 3-3
Oct 28 1911	Bristol Rovers	D 2-2
Nov 11 1911	Northampton Town	D 2-2
Nov 25 1911	Stoke	L 0-1
Dec 9 1911	Leyton	W 2-0

Dec 23 1911	Crystal Palace	W 1-0
Dec 25 1911	Southampton	L 2-3
Dec 30 1911	Reading	D 0-0
Jan 20 1912	New Brompton	W 7-1
Feb 10 1912	Queens Park Rangers	L 1-2
Mar 23 1912	Brighton and Hove Albion	D 1-1
Mar 27 1912	West Ham United	L 1-2
Apr 5 1912	Plymouth Argyle	W 4-0
Apr 6 1912	Coventry City	W 3-0
Apr 20 1912	Norwich City	W 3-0
Apr 24 1912	Swindon Town	W 2-0

F.A. Cup

Nov 18 1911	First Battalion King's Royal Rifles (Fourth Qualifying Round)	D 1-1
Nov 22 1911	First Battalion King's Royal Rifles (Fourth Qualifying Round replay)*	D 1-1
Jan 13 1912	Crystal Palace	D 0-0

Replay at Griffin Park - King's Royal Rifles ground unsuitable.

1912-1913

Southern League Division One

Sep 7 1912	Reading	W 1-0
Sep 18 1912	Crystal Palace	W 2-1
Sep 21 1912	Gillingham	L 0-1
Oct 5 1912	Queens Park Rangers	L 0-2
Oct 26 1912	Bristol Rovers	L 0-1
Nov 9 1912	Portsmouth	W 1-0
Nov 23 1912	West Ham United	W 5-1
Dec 7 1912	Coventry City	W 2-0
Dec 211912	Merthyr Town	W 2-0
Dec 25 1912	Plymouth Argyle	D 2-2
Jan 4 1913	Norwich City	W 1-0
Jan 25 1913	Northampton Town	D 0-0
Feb 15 1913	Stoke	W 4-2
Feb 22 1913	Millwall Athletic	D 0-0
Mar 8 1913	Swindon Town	L 0-3
Mar 21 1913	Southampton	L 1-2
Mar 22 1913	Exeter City	L 0-1
Apr 5 1913	Brighton and Hove Albion	W 4-1
Apr 19 1913	Watford	W 2-0

Southern Alliance

| Oct 16 1912 | Croydon Common | W 4-1 |

Nov 6 1912	Luton Town	D 2-2
Nov 13 1912	Portsmouth	L 1-3
Feb 5 1913	Southampton	W 3-2
Feb 26 1913	Southend United	W 4-0
Apr 9 1913	Brighton and Hove Albion	L 0-2
Apr 14 1913	Cardiff City	W 4-2
Apr 21 1913	Millwall Athletic	L 0-1

F.A. Cup

| Nov 30 1912 | Watford (Fourth Qualifying Round) | D 0-0 |

1913-1914

Southern League Division Two

Sep 20 1913	Caerphilly	W 5-0
Oct 4 1913	Ton Pentre	W 7-0
Oct 18 1913	Swansea Town	W 3-1
Oct 25 1913	Barry	W 5-0
Nov 8 1913	Mardy	W 4-0
Dec 25 1913	Croydon Common	L 0-1
Dec 26 1913	Treharris	W 7-0
Dec 27 1913	Newport County	W 3-0
Jan 17 1914	Stoke	W 2-0
Jan 31 1914	Pontypridd	W 2-0
Feb 14 1914	Llanelly	W 2-0
Mar 14 1914	Mid Rhondda	W 3-1
Mar 28 1814	Abertillery	W 5-0
Apr 10 1914	Aberdare	W 4-0
Apr 11 1914	Luton Town	D 0-0

Southern Alliance

Sep 6 1913	Luton Town	L 2-3
Sep 8 1913	Portsmouth	W 3-1
Sep 15 1913	Cardiff City	D 1-1
Oct 13 1913	Southampton	W 2-0
Nov 10 1913	Croydon Common	L 0-3
Nov 17 1913	Newport County	D 0-0
Jan 12 1914	Southend United	W 2-0
Feb 9 1914	Brighton and Hove Albion	D 1-1

F.A. Cup

| Nov 29 1913 | Luton Clarence (Fourth Qualifying Round) | W 1-0 |
| Dec 13 1913 | Southend United | D 1-1 |

1914-1915

Southern League Division Two

Sep 5 1914	Coventry City	W 3-1
Oct 31 1914	Ebbw Vale	W 3-0
Nov 14 1914	Newport County	W 1-0
Dec 12 1914	Swansea Town	W 2-0
Dec 25 1914	Stoke	D 2-2
Jan 16 1915	Barry	D 0-0
Jan 30 1915	Ton Pentre	D 3-3
Feb 13 1915	Stalybridge Celtic	L 1-3
Mar 13 1915	Llanelly	D 2-2
Mar 27 1915	Mid Rhondda	W 3-1
Apr 2 1915	Merthyr Town	D 1-1
Apr 10 1915	Pontypridd	W 6-0

F.A. Cup

Dec 9 1913	Boscombe (Fifth Qualifying Round replay)	L 0-1

1919-1920

Southern League Division One

Aug 30 1919	Brighton and Hove Albion	W 2-1
Sep 1 1919	Millwall Athletic	D 2-2
Sep 13 1919	Portsmouth	L 0-2
Sep 27 1919	Crystal Palace	D 0-0
Oct 11 1919	Norwich City	D 1-1
Nov 1 1919	Plymouth Argyle	D 0-0
Nov 15 1919	Reading	W 1-0
Nov 29 1919	Luton Town	W 3-1
Dec 13 1919	Swansea Town	D 1-1
Dec 26 1919	Queens Park Rangers	W 2-1
Dec 27 1919	Cardiff City	L 1-2
Jan 17 1920	Newport County	W 2-1
Jan 31 1920	Northampton Town	W 5-0
Feb 14 1920	Southend United	W 2-0
Feb 28 1920	Watford	L 0-3
Mar 6 1920	Merthyr Town	W 3-0
Mar 20 1920	Bristol Rovers	W 3-0
Apr 2 1920	Swindon Town	W 2-0
Apr 3 1920	Southampton	L 2-3
Apr 17 1920	Gillingham	L 1-2

| Apr 26 1920 | Exeter City | W 2-1 |

1920-1921

Football League Division Three (Southern Section)

Aug 30 1920	Millwall	W 1-0
Sep 4 1920	Exeter City	D 0-0
Sep 11 1920	Brighton and Hove Albion	W 2-0
Sep 25 1920	Crystal Palace	L 0-4
Oct 16 1920	Norwich City	W 3-1
Oct 30 1920	Southampton	D 1-1
Nov 13 1920	Bristol Rovers	D 0-0
Nov 27 1920	Reading	W 3-2
Dec 11 1920	Luton Town	W 1-0
Dec 18 1920	Newport County	D 2-2
Dec 25 1920	Queens Park Rangers	L 0-2
Jan 22 1920	Gillingham	D 3-3
Feb 5 1921	Swansea Town	L 1-2
Feb 19 1921	Swindon Town	L 0-1
Mar 5 1921	Portsmouth	L 1-2
Mar 19 1921	Watford	W 1-0
Mar 26 1921	Northampton Town	D 1-1
Mar 28 1921	Grimsby Town	W 5-0
Apr 9 1921	Southend United	D 2-2
Apr 25 1921	Merthyr Town	D 0-0
May 2 1921	Plymouth Argyle	D 0-0

F.A. Cup

| Jan 8 1921 | Huddersfield Town (First Round) | L 1-2 |

1921-22

Football League Division Three (Southern Section)

Aug 27 1921	Merthyr Town	L 0-1
Sep 5 1921	Southend United	W 1-0
Sep 10 1921	Watford	D 1-1
Sep 24 1921	Charlton Athletic	L 0-2
Oct 8 1921	Northampton Town	W 1-0
Oct 22 1921	Queens Park Rangers	W 5-1
Nov 5 1921	Portsmouth	D 2-2
Nov 26 1921	Norwich City	W 2-1
Dec 24 1921	Bristol Rovers	W 4-2
Dec 26 1921	Aberdare Athletic	W 2-1
Jan 14 1922	Southampton	W 1-0

Jan 21 1922	Plymouth Argyle	W 3-1
Feb 4 1922	Newport County	W 1-0
Feb 18 1922	Luton Town	L 0-2
Mar 4 1922	Swindon Town	W 3-0
Mar 25 1922	Gillingham	L 0-1
Apr 8 1922	Millwall	W 1-0
Apr 14 1922	Brighton and Hove Albion	W 4-0
Apr 18 1922	Reading	W 2-0
Apr 22 1922	Exeter City	W 5-2
May 6 1922	Swansea Town	W 3-0

F.A. Cup

Dec 3 1921	Dulwich Hamlet (Fifth Qualifying Round)	W 3-1
Dec 17 1921	Shildon (Sixth Qualifying Round)	W 1-0
Jan 7 1922	Tottenham Hotspur (First Round)	L 0-2

1922-23

Football League Division Three (Southern Section)

Aug 28 1922	Luton Town	W 3-2
Sep 2 1922	Gillingham	W 2-0
Sep 11 1922	Queens Park Rangers	L 1-3
Sep 16 1922	Norwich City	L 1-4
Sep 30 1922	Northampton Town	W 2-1
Oct 14 1922	Exeter City	L 0-1
Oct 28 1922	Brighton and Hove Albion	L 1-2
Nov 4 1922	Merthyr Town	W 3-1
Nov 18 1922	Reading	D 1-1
Dec 23 1922	Bristol Rovers	L 0-1
Dec 26 1922	Watford	W 2-1
Jan 6 1923	Plymouth Argyle	W 2-0
Jan 27 1923	Charlton Athletic	L 0-3
Feb 10 1923	Swindon Town	W 3-0
Feb 24 1923	Aberdare Athletic	L 0-1
Mar 10 1923	Swansea Town	L 0-1
Mar 17 1923	Newport County	D 0-0
Mar 30 1923	Southend United	D 0-0
Mar 31 1923	Bristol City	W 4-0
Apr 14 1923	Portsmouth	W 1-0
Apr 28 1923	Millwall	D 1-1

F.A. Cup

| Dec 6 1922 | Maidstone United (Fifth Qualifying Round replay) | W 4-0 |
| Dec 16 1922 | Merthyr Town (Sixth Qualifying Round) | L 0-1 |

1923-24

Football League Division Three (Southern Section)

Aug 27 1923	Plymouth Argyle	D 1-1
Sep 1 1923	Queens Park Rangers	L 0-1
Sep 8 1923	Luton Town	W 2-1
Sep 22 1923	Brighton and Hove Albion	L 1-2
Oct 13 1923	Bristol Rovers	L 1-2
Oct 27 1923	Southend United	W 3-1
Nov 10 1923	Portsmouth	D 1-1
Nov 24 1923	Exeter City	W 1-0
Dec 8 1923	Aberdare Athletic	D 1-1
Dec 22 1923	Gillingham	W 3-2
Dec 26 1923	Bournemouth & Boscombe Athletic	W 2-0
Jan 5 1924	Millwall	L 1-3
Jan 26 1924	Newport County	D 0-0
Feb 9 1924	Merthyr Town	D 0-0
Feb 23 1924	Charlton Athletic	D 0-0
Mar 8 1924	Norwich City	W 3-0
Mar 15 1924	Swindon Town	D 2-2
Mar 29 1924	Watford	W 4-1
Apr 12 1924	Swansea Town	D 2-2
Apr 21 1924	Reading	W 4-1
Apr 26 1924	Northampton Town	W 1-0

F.A. Cup

Dec 5 1923	Botwell Mission	
	(Fifth Qualifying Round replay)	W 2-0
Dec 15 1923	Portsmouth (Sixth Qualifying Round)	D 1-1

1924-25

Football League Division Three (Southern Section)

Aug 30 1924	Brighton and Hove Albion	L 2-4
Sep 8 1924	Gillingham	W 2-1
Sep 13 1924	Bristol City	W 1-0
Sep 15 1924	Newport County	W 2-0
Sep 27 1924	Aberdare Athletic	D 2-2
Oct 11 1924	Queens Park Rangers	L 0-1
Oct 18 1924	Millwall	W 1-0
Nov 1 1924	Reading	L 0-1
Nov 15 1924	Exeter City	L 2-5
Dec 13 1924	Watford	D 0-0
Dec 26 1924	Charlton Athletic	W 1-0

Jan 3 1925	Plymouth Argyle	W 1-0
Jan 10 1925	Southend United	D 2-2
Jan 24 1925	Swindon Town	D 0-0
Feb 7 1925	Norwich City	D 1-1
Feb 28 1925	Merthyr Town	D 2-2
Mar 14 1925	Swansea Town	W 3-1
Mar 28 1925	Bristol Rovers	D 1-1
Apr 10 1925	Luton Town	W 3-0
Apr 25 1925	Northampton Town	L 1-3
May 2 1925	Bournemouth & Boscombe Athletic	L 1-2

1925-26

Football League Division Three (Southern Section)

Aug 29 1925	Northampton Town	L 3-4
Sep 7 1925	Southend United	L 1-3
Sep 12 1925	Brighton and Hove Albion	L 1-6
2Sep 6 1925	Queens Park Rangers	L 1-2
Oct 24 1925	Swindon Town	W 3-1
Nov 7 1925	Luton Town	W 1-0
Nov 21 1925	Charlton Athletic	W 4-0
Dec 5 1925	Merthyr Town	D 1-1
Dec 19 1925	Reading	W 1-0
Dec 26 1925	Millwall	W 2-0
Jan 16 1926	Aberdare Athletic	W 1-0
Jan 30 1926	Watford	W 4-3
Feb 13 1926	Crystal Palace	W 3-2
Feb 20 1926	Bristol City	W 2-1
Feb 27 1926	Bristol Rovers	W 4-1
Mar 13 1926	Newport County	D 3-3
Mar 27 1926	Bournemouth and Boscombe Athletic	L 0-2
Apr 2 1926	Norwich City	W 5-1
Apr 10 1926	Gillingham	D 0-0
Apr 24 1926	Exeter City	W 2-0
Apr 26 1926	Plymouth Argyle	D 2-2

F.A. Cup

Nov 28 1925	Barnet (First Round)	W 3-1
Dec 12 1925	Bournemouth and Boscombe Athletic (Second Round)	L 1-2

1926-27

Football League Division Three (Southern Section)

Aug 28 1926	Brighton and Hove Albion	W 4-0
Sep 6 1926	Southend United	W 3-1
Sep 11 1926	Queens Park Rangers	W 4-2
Sep 18 1926	Millwall	D 0-0
Oct 2 1926	Swindon Town	D 2-2
Oct 23 1926	Coventry City	W 7-3
Nov 6 1926	Bristol City	W 3-0
Nov 20 1926	Plymouth Argyle	D 0-0
Dec 4 1926	Aberdare Athletic	L 1-4
Dec 18 1926	Watford	W 3-0
Dec 27 1926	Norwich City	W 3-0
Jan 1 1927	Luton Town	D 2-2
Jan 22 1927	Northampton Town	D 1-1
Feb 12 1927	Bristol Rovers	L 0-2
Feb 26 1927	Exeter City	W 6-1
Mar 5 1927	Crystal Palace	W 3-0
Mar 19 1927	Charlton Athletic	W 2-0
Apr 2 1927	Bournemouth & Boscombe Athletic	D 0-0
Apr 15 1927	Merthyr Town	D 1-1
Apr 16 1927	Newport County	D 1-1
Apr 30 1927	Gillingham	D 0-0

F.A. Cup

Dec 1 1926	Clapton (First Round replay)	W 7-3
Dec 15 1926	Gillingham (Second Round replay)	W 1-0
Feb 2 1927	West Ham United (Fourth Round replay)	W 2-0

1927-28

Football League Division Three (Southern Section)

Aug 29 1927	Northampton Town	W 3-0
Sep 3 1927	Bournemouth & Boscombe Athletic	W 2-1
Sep 24 1927	Millwall	W 6-1
Oct 8 1927	Exeter City	D 1-1
Oct 22 1927	Coventry City	W 4-1
Nov 5 1927	Swindon Town	L 1-4
Dec 3 1927	Plymouth Argyle	L 0-2
Dec 5 1927	Walsall	W 3-2
Dec 17 1927	Charlton Athletic	D 1-1
Dec 31 1927	Brighton and Hove Albion	L 1-3
Jan 21 1928	Queens Park Rangers	L 0-3
Jan 28 1928	Luton Town	W 4-2
Feb 11 1928	Crystal Palace	W 2-1
Feb 25 1928	Torquay United	L 1-2
Mar 10 1928	Newport County	W 3-1
Mar 24 1928	Gillingham	W 2-0

Apr 6 1928	Norwich City	W 3-1
Apr 7 1928	Bristol Rovers	W 5-1
Apr 21 1928	Merthyr Town	W 4-0
Apr 23 1928	Southend United	D 2-2
May 5 1928	Watford	D 1-1

1928-29

Football League Division Three (Southern Section)

Aug 25 1928	Exeter City	W 4-2
Sep 3 1928	Charlton Athletic	W 1-0
Sep 8 1928	Merthyr Town	W 2-1
Sep 10 1928	Swindon Town	W 2-0
Sep 22 1928	Queens Park Rangers	D 1-1
2Sep 9 1928	Luton Town	L 0-1
Oct 13 1928	Northampton Town	D 2-2
Oct 27 1928	Watford	L 0-1
Nov 10 1928	Newport County	L 1-3
Dec 22 1928	Fulham	L 1-2
Dec 26 1928	Brighton and Hove Albion	W 5-1
Jan 5 1929	Southend United	W 1-0
Jan 12 1929	Gillingham	W 4-1
Feb 16 1929	Coventry City	W 1-0
Mar 2 1929	Bristol Rovers	W 2-0
Mar 13 1929	Bournemouth & Boscombe Athletic	D 0-0
Mar 16 1929	Walsall	W 1-0
Mar 29 1929	Norwich City	W 4-0
Mar 30 1929	Crystal Palace	L 2-4
Apr 13 1929	Torquay United	D 0-0
Apr 27 1929	Plymouth Argyle	L 0-2

F.A. Cup

| Nov 24 1928 | Brighton and Hove Albion (First Round) | W 4-1 |
| Dec 8 1928 | Plymouth Argyle (Second Round) | L 0-1 |

1929-30

Football League Division Three (Southern Section)

Aug 31 1929	Swindon Town	W 3-2
Sep 4 1929	Clapton Orient	W 3-1
Sep 14 1929	Merthyr Town	W 6-0
Sep 25 1929	Bristol Rovers	W 2-1
Sep 28 1929	Newport County	W 1-0
Oct 12 1929	Coventry City	W 3-1

Oct 26 1929	Norwich City	W 3-0
Nov 9 1929	Gillingham	W 2-1
Nov 23 1929	Exeter City	W 2-0
Dec 7 1929	Luton Town	W 2-0
Dec 21 1929	Walsall	W 6-2
Dec 25 1929	Brighton and Hove Albion	W 5-2
Jan 4 1930	Plymouth Argyle	W 3-0
Jan 25 1930	Torquay United	W 5-0
Feb 8 1930	Watford	W 5-0
Feb 22 1930	Fulham	W 5-1
Mar 8 1930	Crystal Palace	W 2-0
Mar 22 193	Northampton Town	W 2-0
Apr 5 1930	Southend United	W 2-1
Apr 19 1930	Bournemouth & Boscombe Athletic	W 1-0
Apr 21 1930	Queens Park Rangers	W 3-0

1930-1931

Football League Division Three (Southern Section)

Sep 3 1930	Northampton Town	L 0-4
Sep 6 1930	Bristol Rovers	W 4-0
Sep 17 1930	Fulham	W 4-1
Sep 20 1930	Gillingham	D 1-1
Sep 24 1930	Notts County	D 2-2
Oct 4 1930	Brighton and Hove Albion	W 3-2
Oct 18 1930	Coventry City	L 1-2
Nov 1 1930	Queens Park Rangers	W 5-3
Nov 15 1930	Thames	W 6-1
Dec 18 1930	Bournemouth & Boscombe Athletic	L 1-2
Dec 25 1930	Crystal Palace	W 8-2
Dec 27 1930	Luton Town	L 0-1
Jan 17 1931	Newport County	W 3-2
Jan 31 1931	Exeter City	W 2-1
Feb 14 1931	Torquay United	D 0-0
Feb 28 1931	Walsall	W 6-1
Mar 14 1931	Norwich City	W 3-1
Mar 28 1931	Clapton Orient	W 3-0
Apr 2 1931	Southend United	W 3-1
Apr 11 1931	Watford	W 2-1
Apr 25 1931	Swindon Town	W 5-2

F.A. Cup

Dec 13 1930	Norwich City (Second Round)	W 1-0
Jan 10 1931	Cardiff City (Third Round)	D 2-2
Jan 24 1931	Portsmouth (Fourth Round)	L 0-1

1931-1932

Football League Division Three (Southern Section)

Aug 29 1931	Queens Park Rangers	W 1-0
Sep 12 1931	Coventry City	W 4-2
Sep 24 1931	Reading	W 3-0
Sep 26 1931	Luton Town	W 1-0
Oct 10 1931	Northampton Town	W 2-0
Oct 17 1931	Bristol Rovers	W 4-2
Oct 31 1931	Clapton Orient	W 3-0
Nov 14 1931	Norwich City	L 0-1
Dec 25 1931	Fulham	D 0-0
Jan 13 1932	Mansfield Town	D 1-1
Jan 16 1932	Exeter City	D 2-2
Jan 30 1932	Gillingham	D 1-1
Feb 13 1932	Cardiff City	L 2-3
Mar 5 1932	Torquay United	W 3-0
Mar 19 1932	Swindon Town	W 2-0
Mar 25 1932	Southend United	L 2-3
Apr 2 1932	Brighton and Hove Albion	D 2-2
Apr 13 1932	Crystal Palace	D 1-1
Apr 16 1932	Watford	L 1-2
Apr 30 1932	Bournemouth & Boscombe Athletic	W 4-2
May 7 1932	Thames	W 1-0

F.A. Cup

Dec 2 1931	Tunbridge Wells Rangers (First Round replay)	W 2-1
Dec 12 1931	Norwich City (Second Round)	W 4-1
Jan 9 1932	Bath City (Third Round)	W 2-0

1932-1933

Football League Division Three (Southern Section)

Sep 3 1932	Torquay United	W 3-1
Sep 8 1932	Coventry City	W 2-1
Sep 17 1932	Luton Town	W 1-0
Oct 1 1932	Bournemouth and Boscombe Athletic	D 1-1
Oct 15 1932	Clapton Orient	W 4-2
Oct 29 1932	Crystal Palace	W 2-0
Nov 12 1932	Watford	W 2-1
Dec 24 1932	Aldershot Town	W 2-0
Dec 27 1932	Northampton Town	W 1-0
Dec 31 1932	Queens Park Rangers	W 2-0

Jan 21 1933	Exeter City	L 0-2
Feb 4 1933	Newport County	W 6-0
Feb 18 1933	Swindon Town	W 1-0
Mar 4 1933	Southend United	W 3-1
Mar 18 1933	Gillingham	L 1-2
Apr 1 1933	Cardiff City	W 7-3
Apr 15 1933	Norwich City	D 2-2
Apr 17 1933	Bristol City	W 2-1
Apr 26 1933	Brighton and Hove Albion	W 2-1
Apr 29 1933	Bristol Rovers	D 0-0
May 3 1933	Reading	D 1-1

1933-1934

Football League Division Two

Aug 31 1933	Bradford Park Avenue	W 2-0
Sep 2 1933	West Ham United	W 4-1
Sep 16 1933	Manchester United	L 3-4
Sep 30 1933	Hull City	D 2-2
Oct 7 1933	Burnley	W 5-2
Oct 28 1933	Southampton	W 2-0
Nov 11 1933	Bradford City	W 2-1
Nov 25 1933	Notts County	D 2-2
Dec 9 1933	Millwall	W 3-0
Dec 23 1933	Bury	L 2-3
Dec 25 1933	Preston North End	W 3-2
Dec 30 1933	Nottingham Forest	W 2-1
Jan 20 1934	Plymouth Argyle	W 3-0
Feb 3 1934	Bolton Wanderers	W 3-1
Feb 24 1934	Oldham Athletic	W 2-1
Mar 3 1934	Fulham	L 1-2
Mar 17 1934	Blackpool	W 1-0
Mar 31 1934	Port Vale	W 2-0
Apr 2 1934	Grimsby Town	L 1-2
Apr 14 1934	Swansea Town	W 2-0
Apr 28 1934	Lincoln City	W 5-0

1934-1935

Football League Division Two

Aug 25 1934	Norwich City	W 2-1
Sep 5 1934	Fulham	W 1-0
Sep 8 1934	West Ham United	W 4-1
Sep 22 1934	Bury	W 2-1
Oct 6 1934	Nottingham Forest	D 1-1

Oct 20 1934	Notts County	W 4-1
Nov 3 1934	Bolton Wanderers	W 1-0
Nov 17 1934	Burnley	W 6-1
Dec 1 1934	Manchester United	W 3-1
Dec 15 1934	Barnsley	W 8-1
Dec 25 1934	Plymouth Argyle	D 0-0
Jan 5 1935	Newcastle United	W 3-0
Jan 26 1935	Blackpool	W 2-1
Feb 9 1935	Hull City	W 2-1
Feb 23 1935	Bradford City	W 2-0
Mar 9 1935	Southampton	W 3-2
Mar 23 1935	Oldham Athletic	W 2-1
Apr 6 1935	Swansea Town	W 1-0
Apr 19 1935	Bradford Park Avenue	W 1-0
Apr 20 1935	Port Vale	W 8-0
May 4 1935	Sheffield United	W 3-1

F.A. Cup

Jan 12 1935	Plymouth Argyle (Third Round)	L 0-1

1935-1936

Football League Division One

Sep 5 1935	Blackburn Rovers	W 3-1
Sep 7 1935	Huddersfield Town	L 1-2
Sep 21 1935	Aston Villa	L 1-2
Oct 5 1935	Sheffield Wednesday	D 2-2
Oct 19 1935	Stoke City	D 0-0
Nov 2 1935	Arsenal	W 2-1
Nov 16 1935	Sunderland	L 1-5
Nov 30 1935	Leeds United	D 2-2
Dec 14 1935	Liverpool	L 1-2
Dec 25 1935	Preston North End	W 5-2
Dec 28 1935	Bolton Wanderers	W 4-0
Jan 18 1936	Middlesbrough	W 1-0
Feb 1 1936	Wolverhampton Wanderers	W 5-0
Feb 29 1936	Birmingham	L 0-1
Mar 14 1936	Manchester City	D 0-0
Mar 25 1936	Portsmouth	W 3-1
Mar 28 1936	Chelsea	W 2-1
Apr 11 1936	Grimsby Town	W 3-0
Apr 13 1936	Everton	W 4-1
Apr 25 1936	West Bromwich Albion	D 2-2
May 2 1936	Derby County	W 6-0

1936-1937

Football League Division One

Aug 29 1936	Bolton Wanderers	D 2-2
Sep 3 1936	Arsenal	W 2-0
Sep 12 1936	Huddersfield Town	D 1-1
Sep 17 1936	Charlton Athletic	W 4-2
Sep 26 1936	Wolverhampton Wanderers	W 3-2
Oct 10 1936	Manchester United	W 4-0
Oct 24 1936	Liverpool	W 5-2
Nov 7 1936	Birmingham	W 2-1
Nov 21 1936	West Bromwich Albion	W 2-1
Dec 5 1936	Portsmouth	W 4-0
Dec 19 1936	Stoke City	W 2-1
Dec 25 1936	Sheffield Wednesday	W 2-1
Jan 2 1937	Everton	D 2-2
Jan 23 1937	Sunderland	D 3-3
Feb 6 1937	Derby County	W 6-2
Mar 3 1937	Grimsby Town	L 2-3
Mar 6 1937	Leeds United	W 4-1
Mar 20 1937	Middlesbrough	W 4-1
Mar 26 1937	Preston North End	D 1-1
Apr 3 1937	Manchester City	L 2-6
Apr 17 1937	Chelsea	W 1-0

F.A. Cup

| Jan 16 1937 | Huddersfield Town (Third Round) | W 5-0 |

1937-1938

Football League Division One

Sep 1 1937	Preston North End	W 2-1
Sep 4 1937	Huddersfield Town	W 2-0
Sep 16 1937	Blackpool	L 2-4
Sep 18 1937	Wolverhampton Wanderers	W 2-1
Oct 2 1937	Sunderland	W 4-0
Oct 16 1937	Charlton Athletic	W 5-2
Oct 30 1937	Portsmouth	W 2-0
Nov 13 1937	Middlesbrough	D 3-3
Nov 27 1937	West Bromwich Albion	L 0-2
Dec 11 1937	Leeds United	D 1-1
Dec 27 1937	Manchester City	W 2-1
Jan 1 1938	Bolton Wanderers	D 1-1
Jan 26 1938	Everton	W 3-0
Feb 5 1938	Leicester City	D 1-1

Feb 19 1938	Derby County	L 2-3
Mar 9 1938	Chelsea	D 1-1
Mar 19 1938	Liverpool	L 1-3
Apr 2 1938	Grimsby Town	W 6-1
Apr 16 1938	Stoke City	D 0-0
Apr 18 1938	Arsenal	W 3-0
Apr 30 1938	Birmingham	L 1-2

F.A. Cup

Jan 8 1938	Fulham (Third Round)	W 3-1
Jan 22 1938	Portsmouth (Fourth Round)	W 2-1
Feb 12 1938	Manchester United (Fifth Round)	W 2-0
Mar 5 1938	Preston North End (Sixth Round)	L 0-3

1938-1939

Football League Division One

Aug 27 1938	Huddersfield Town	W 2-1
Sep 8 1938	Arsenal	W 1-0
Sep 10 1938	Wolverhampton Wanderers	L 0-1
Sep 24 1938	Sunderland	L 2-3
Oct 8 1938	Derby County	L 1-3
Oct 22 1938	Chelsea	W 1-0
Nov 5 1938	Bolton Wanderers	D 2-2
Nov 19 1938	Liverpool	W 2-1
Dec 3 1938	Middlesbrough	W 2-1
Dec 17 1938	Manchester United	L 2-5
Dec 31 1938	Everton	W 2-0
Feb 4 1939	Grimsby Town	L 1-2
Feb 7 1939	Aston Villa	L 2-4
Feb 18 1939	Stoke City	W 1-0
Feb 22 1939	Portsmouth	W 2-0
Mar 4 1939	Charlton Athletic	W 1-0
Mar 18 1939	Leeds United	L 0-1
Apr 1 1939	Leicester City	W 2-0
Apr 7 1939	Preston North End	W 3-1
Apr 15 1939	Birmingham	L 0-1
Apr 29 1939	Blackpool	D 1-1

F.A. Cup

| Jan 7 1939 | Newcastle United (Third Round) | L 0-2 |

1945-46

No League competition - F.A. Cup on a two-legged basis for one season.

F.A. Cup

Jan 10 1946	Tottenham Hotspur (Third Round - Second leg)	W 2-0
Jan 31 1946	Bristol City (Fourth Round - Second leg)	W 5-0
Feb 14 1946	Queens Park Rangers (Fifth Round - Second leg)	D 0-0
Mar 9 1946	Charlton Athletic (Sixth Round - Second leg)	L 1-3

1946-1947

Football League Division One

Sep 7 1946	Huddersfield Town	W 2-0
Sep 18 1946	Blackpool	W 2-1
Sep 21 1946	Sunderland	L 0-3
Oct 5 1946	Derby County	L 0-3
Oct 19 1946	Preston North End	L 2-3
Nov 2 1946	Bolton Wanderers	W 1-0
Nov 16 1946	Charlton Athletic	L 1-4
Nov 30 1946	Leeds United	D 1-1
Dec 14 1946	Stoke City	L 1-4
Dec 26 1946	Sheffield United	W 2-1
Dec 28 1946	Everton	D 1-1
Jan 18 1947	Wolverhampton Wanderers	W 4-1
Feb 1 1947	Aston Villa	L 0-2
Mar 15 1947	Chelsea	L 0-2
Mar 29 1947	Grimsby Town	L 0-1
Apr 4 1947	Portsmouth	L 1-3
Apr 12 1947	Manchester United	D 0-0
Apr 26 1947	Middlesbrough	D 0-0
May 3 1947	Blackburn Rovers	L 0-3
May 17 1947	Liverpool	D 1-1
May 26 1947	Arsenal	L 0-1

F.A. Cup

Jan 11 1947	Cardiff City (Third Round)	W 1-0
Jan 25 1947	Leicester City (Fourth Round)	D 0-0

1947-1948

Football League Division Two

Aug 27 1947	Luton Town	L 0-3
Aug 30 1947	Coventry City	L 1-4
Sep 10 1947	Nottingham Forest	W 3-1
Sep 13 1947	Birmingham Cit	L 1-2
Sep 27 1947	Barnsley	D 3-3
Oct 11 1947	Bradford Park Avenue	W 2-1
Oct 18 1947	Cardiff City	D 0-0
Oct 25 1947	Sheffield Wednesday	W 1-0
Nov 8 1947	Millwall	W 2-1
Nov 22 1947	West Ham United	D 1-1
Dec 6 1947	Southampton	D 2-2
Dec 20 1947	Fulham	L 0-2
Dec 25 1947	Leicester City	D 2-2
Jan 17 1948	Newcastle United	W 1-0
Feb 7 1948	West Bromwich Albion	W 1-0
Feb 21 1948	Plymouth Argyle	D 0-0
Mar 20 1948	Tottenham Hotspur	W 2-0
Mar 26 1948	Leeds United	W 3-0
Apr 3 1948	Chesterfield	L 0-3
Apr 17 1948	Bury	W 4-1
May 1 1948	Doncaster Rovers	W 2-0

F.A. Cup

Jan 24 1948	Middlesbrough (Fourth round)	L 1-2

1948-1949

Football League Division Two

Aug 21 1948	Coventry City	D 2-2
Sep 1 1948	Leeds United	L 1-3
Sep 4 1948	Lincoln City	W 2-1
Sep 15 1948	Leicester City	L 1-2
Sep 18 1948	West Bromwich Albion	D 0-0
Oct 2 1948	West Ham United	D 0-0
Oct 16 1948	Luton Town	W 2-0
Oct 30 1948	Southampton	D 0-0
Nov 13 1948	Grimsby Town	W 2-0
Dec 11 1948	Blackburn Rovers	L 0-1
Dec 25 1948	Cardiff City	D 1-1
Jan 1 1949	Sheffield Wednesday	W 2-1
Jan 22 1949	Chesterfield	D 1-1
Feb 19 1949	Bury	W 8-2

Mar 5 1949	Queens Park Rangers	L 0-3
Mar 19 1949	Bradford Park Avenue	W 1-0
Apr 2 1949	Barnsley	D 0-0
Apr 6 1949	Fulham	D 0-0
Apr 16 1949	Nottingham Forest	W 2-1

F.A. Cup

Jan 8 1949	Middlesbrough (Third round)	W 3-2
Jan 29 1949	Torquay United (Fourth Round)	W 1-0
Feb 12 1949	Burnley (Fifth Round)	W 4-2
Feb 26 1949	Leciester City (Sixth Round)	L 0-2

1949-1950

Football League Division Two

Apr 18 1949	Tottenham Hotspur	D 1-1
Apr 30 1949	Plymouth Argyle	D 2-2
Aug 20 1949	Tottenham Hotspur	L 1-4
Aug 31 1949	Queens Park Rangers	L 0-2
Sep 3 1949	Leicester City	L 0-1
Sep 14 1949	Blackburn Rovers	W 2-0
Sep 17 1949	Chesterfield	D 0-0
Oct 1 1949	Sheffield Wednesday	D 1-1
Oct 15 1949	Swansea Town	D 0-0
Oct 29 1949	Southampton	L 0-1
Nov 12 1949	Luton Town	W 1-0
Nov 26 1949	West Ham United	L 0-2
Dec 10 1949	Grimsby Town	W 1-0
Dec 24 1949	Bury	W 2-0
Dec 26 1949	Hull City	W 3-1
Jan 14 1950	Bradford Park Avenue	W 2-0
Feb 4 1950	Plymouth Argyle	D 0-0
Feb 25 1950	Preston North End	W 1-0
Mar 11 1950	Leeds United	D 0-0
Mar 25 1950	Coventry City	W 2-0
Apr 7 1950	Cardiff City	W 1-0
Apr 8 1950	Sheffield United	W 1-0
Apr 22 1950	Barnsley	W 3-0

F.A. Cup

| Jan 7 1950 | Chelsea (Third Round) | L 0-1 |

1950-1951

Football League Division Two

Aug 26 1950	Leeds United	L 1-2
Aug 30 1950	Blackburn Rovers	W 3-2
Sep 9 1950	Swansea Town	W 2-1
Sep 13 1950	Barnsley	L 0-2
Sep 23 1950	Doncaster Rovers	D 1-1
Oct 7 1950	Coventry City	L 0-4
Oct 21 1950	Birmingham City	W 2-1
Nov 4 1950	Notts County	L 1-3
Nov 18 1950	Leicester City	D 0-0
Dec 2 1950	Queens Park Rangers	W 2-1
Dec 16 1950	Luton Town	W 1-0
Dec 26 1950	Southampton	W 4-0
Dec 30 1950	West Ham United	D 1-1
Jan 20 1951	Hull City	W 2-1
Feb 10 1951	Bury	W 4-0
Feb 17 1951	Preston North End	L 2-4
Mar 3 1951	Manchester City	W 2-0
Mar 17 1951	Cardiff City	W 4-0
Mar 23 1951	Sheffield United	W 3-1
Mar 31 1951	Grimsby Town	W 5-1
Apr 14 1951	Chesterfield	W 4-0

1951-52

Football League Division Two

Aug 25 1951	Rotherham United	W 2-0
Aug 27 1951	Everton	W 1-0
Sep 8 1951	Birmingham City	W 1-0
Sep 22 1951	Nottingham Forest	D 1-1
Oct 6 1951	Notts County	W 1-0
Oct 20 1951	Bury	W 4-0
Nov 3 1951	Coventry City	W 1-0
Nov 17 1951	Sheffield United	W 4-1
Dec 1 1951	Hull City	W 2-1
Dec 15 1951	Leeds United	W 2-1
Dec 25 1951	Southampton	L 1-2
Dec 29 1951	Cardiff City	D 1-1
Jan 19 1952	Leicester City	L 1-3
Feb 9 1952	Queens Park Rangers	D 0-0
Mar 1 1952	Luton Town	D 3-3
Mar 15 1952	Swansea Town	W 3-1
Apr 11 1952	Sheffield Wednesday	L 2-3
Apr 12 1952	Barnsley	D 1-1
Apr 21 1952	West Ham United	D 1-1
Apr 26 1952	Blackburn Rovers	D 1-1

| Apr 30 1952 | Doncaster Rovers | W 1-0 |

F.A. Cup

| Jan 12 1952 | Queens Park Rangers (Third Round) | W 3-1 |
| Feb 6 1952 | Luton Town (Fourth Round replay) | D 0-0 |

1952-1953

Football League Division Two

Aug 23 1952	Lincoln City	W 1-0
Sep 3 1952	Huddersfield Town	L 1-3
Sep 6 1952	Blackburn Rovers	W 3-2
Sep 17 1952	Sheffield United	D 0-0
Sep 20 1952	Everton	L 2-4
Oct 11 1952	Southampton	W 3-0
Oct 25 1952	Leicester City	W 4-2
Nov 8 1952	Fulham	D 2-2
Nov 22 1952	Plymouth Argyle	L 1-2
Dec 25 1952	Barnsley	W 4-0
Jan 3 1953	Hull City	W 1-0
Jan 24 1953	Nottingham Forest	D 1-1
Feb 14 1953	Bury	D 2-2
Feb 21 1953	Doncaster Rovers	W 1-0
Mar 7 1953	Notts County	W 5-0
Mar 21 1953	West Ham United	L 1-4
Apr 3 1953	Swansea Town	D 0-0
Apr 4 1953	Rotherham United	D 1-1
Apr 18 1953	Leeds United	D 3-3
Apr 22 1953	Luton Town	D 1-1
May 1 1953	Birmingham City	L 1-2

F.A. Cup

| Jan 10 1953 | Leeds United (Third round) | W 2-1 |
| Feb 4 1954 | Aston Villa (Fourth Round replay) | L 1-2 |

1953-1954

Football League Division Two

Aug 27 1953	Blackburn Rovers	L 1-4
Aug 29 1953	Fulham	W 2-1
Sep 5 1953	Bristol Rovers	L 0-3
Sep 10 1953	Doncaster Rovers	L 1-4

Sep 19 1953	Notts County	D 0-0
Oct 3 1953	Everton	W 1-0
Oct 17 1953	Leeds United	W 2-1
Oct 31 1953	Nottingham Forest	D 1-1
Nov 14 1953	Plymouth Argyle	W 1-0
Nov 28 1953	Rotherham United	L 0-1
Dec 12 1953	Stoke City	D 0-0
Dec 19 1953	Derby County	D 0-0
Dec 25 1953	Oldham Athletic	W 3-1
Jan 23 1954	Lincoln City	L 0-1
Feb 13 1954	Hull City	D 2-2
Feb 27 1954	West Ham United	W 3-1
Mar 13 1954	Birmingham City	W 2-0
Mar 27 1954	Swansea Town	W 3-1
Apr 10 1954	Luton Town	L 0-1
Apr 16 1954	Bury	W 2-1
Apr 24 1954	Leicester City	L 1-3

F.A. Cup

| Jan 9 1954 | Hull City (Third Round) | D 0-0 |

1954-1955

Football League Division Three (Southern Section)

Aug 26 1954	Shrewsbury Town	D 2-2
Aug 28 1954	Coventry City	L 2-3
Sep 4 1954	Queens Park Rangers	D 1-1
Sep 16 1954	Reading	D 2-2
Sep 18 1954	Torquay United	W 4-2
Sep 23 1954	Gillingham	W 3-0
Oct 2 1954	Walsall	L 0-2
Oct 16 1954	Colchester United	W 3-2
Oct 30 1954	Bournemouth and Boscombe Athletic	L 1-3
Nov 13 1954	Swindon Town	W 4-2
Nov 27 1954	Northampton Town	L 1-3
Dec 18 1954	Southampton	L 0-3
Dec 25 1954	Millwall	W 3-1
Jan 22 1955	Brighton and Hove Albion	L 2-3
Feb 12 1955	Bristol City	D 2-2
Feb 26 1955	Exeter City	W 1-0
Mar 12 1955	Norwich City	W 1-0
Mar 26 1955	Aldershot	D 1-1
Apr 8 1955	Leyton Orient	W 2-0
Apr 9 1955	Crystal Palace	W 3-0
Apr 23 1955	Watford	W 3-2
May 2 1955	Newport County	W 1-0

| May 5 1955 | Southend United | D 2-2 |

F.A. Cup

Nov 20 1954	Nuneaton Borough (First Round)	W 2-1
Dec 11 1954	Crook Town (Second Round)	W 4-1
Jan 8 1955	Bradford City (Third Round)	D 1-1

1955-1956

Football League Division Three (Southern Section)

Aug 20 1955	Gillingham	L 1-4
Aug 30 1955	Queens Park Rangers	W 2-0
Sep 3 1955	Norwich City	L 1-2
Sep 12 1955	Millwall	D 2-2
Sep 17 1955	Leyton Orient	W 1-0
Sep 19 1955	Watford	D 0-0
Oct 1 1955	Southend United	W 2-1
Oct 15 1955	Crystal Palace	W 3-0
Oct 29 1955	Southampton	W 2-1
Nov 12 1955	Ipswich Town	W 3-2
Nov 26 1955	Torquay United	L 1-3
Dec 24 1955	Bournemouth and Boscombe Athletic	W 2-1
Dec 26 1955	Reading	D 2-2
Jan 14 1956	Colchester United	D 2-2
Feb 4 1956	Exeter City	W 2-0
Feb 18 1956	Aldershot	W 2-0
Mar 3 1956	Brighton and Hove Albion	W 4-2
Mar 12 1956	Swindon Town	L 1-2
Mar 17 1956	Shrewsbury Town	D 1-1
Mar 31 1956	Walsall	D 2-2
Apr 2 1956	Northampton Town	W 2-1
Apr 14 1956	Newport County	D 1-1
Apr 23 1956	Coventry City	D 1-1
Aug 18 1956	Plymouth Argyle	W 4-1
Aug 21 1956	Swindon Town	W 4-1

F.A. Cup

| Nov 19 1955 | March Town (First Round) | W 4-0 |

1956-1957

Football League Division Three (Southern Section)

| Sep 1 1956 | Watford | L 1-5 |

Sep 4 1956	Brighton and Hove Albion	L 2-5
Sep 15 1956	Walsall	W 6-2
Sep 18 1956	Gillingham	W 3-2
Sep 29 1956	Bournemouth and Boscombe Athletic	D 2-2
Oct 6 1956	Northampton Town	W 2-1
Oct 20 1956	Crystal Palace	D 1-1
Nov 3 1956	Southampton	W 4-0
Dec 1 1956	Newport County	D 0-0
Dec 22 1956	Aldershot	D 2-2
Dec 25 1956	Torquay United	D 0-0
Jan 12 1957	Shrewsbury Town	W 3-1
Feb 2 1957	Ipswich Town	D 1-1
Mar 4 1957	Millwall	W 5-0
Mar 9 1957	Reading	W 4-0
Mar 12 1957	Southend United	W 3-2
Mar 23 1957	Coventry City	D 1-1
Apr 6 1957	Colchester United	D 1-1
Apr 19 1957	Queens Park Rangers	W 2-0
Apr 20 1957	Exeter City	W 3-0
Apr 27 1957	Norwich City	D 1-1

F.A. Cup

| Nov 17 1956 | Guildford City (First Round) | W 3-0 |
| Dec 8 1956 | Crystal Palace (Second Round) | D 1-1 |

1957-1958

Football League Division Three (Southern Section)

Aug 27 1957	Exeter City	W 1-0
Aug 31 1957	Colchester United	D 3-3
Sep 10 1957	Northampton Town	W 7-1
Sep 14 1957	Bournemouth and Boscombe Athletic	W 4-2
Sep 28 1957	Coventry City	L 1-3
Oct 1 1957	Watford	D 0-0
Oct 12 1957	Gillingham	W 1-0
Oct 26 1957	Swindon Town	D 0-0
Nov 9 1957	Plymouth Argyle	W 2-0
Nov 23 1957	Newport County	W 2-1
Dec 21 1957	Queens Park Rangers	D 1-1
Dec 25 1957	Crystal Palace	L 0-3
Jan 11 1958	Norwich City	W 7-1
Feb 1 1958	Walsall	W 2-1
Feb 15 1958	Shrewsbury Town	W 2-0
Mar 1 1958	Millwall	W 4-1
Mar 11 1958	Reading	W 2-1
Mar 15 1958	Aldershot	W 4-2

Mar 29 1958	Southend United	W 4-2
Apr 7 1958	Torquay United	L 0-1
Apr 12 1958	Southampton	D 0-0
Apr 26 1958	Port Vale	W 4-1
Apr 28 1958	Brighton and Hove Albion	W 1-0

1958-1959

Football League Division Three

Aug 23 1958	Bradford City	W 4-0
Sep 2 1958	Doncaster Rovers	L 0-1
Sep 6 1958	Southampton	W 2-0
Sep 9 1958	Mansfield Town	W 2-0
Sep 20 1958	Halifax Town	W 2-0
Sep 30 1958	Hull City	D 1-1
Oct 4 1958	Chesterfield	D 1-1
Oct 18 1958	Stockport County	L 1-4
Nov 1 1958	Colchester United	W 2-1
Nov 29 1958	Bury	D 0-0
Dec 13 1958	Rochdale	W 2-1
Dec 25 1958	Swindon Town	D 2-2
Jan 3 1959	Wrexham	W 2-1
Jan 31 1959	Accrington Stanley	W 2-1
Feb 14 1959	Newport County	W 3-0
Feb 28 1959	Tranmere Rovers	W 5-2
Mar 14 1959	Reading	W 3-1
Mar 27 1959	Plymouth Argyle	W 3-0
Mar 28 1959	Bournemouth and Boscombe Athletic	D 1-1
Apr 11 1959	Queens Park Rangers	W 1-0
Apr 21 1959	Notts County	W 4-0
Apr 25 1959	Southend United	W 6-1
Apr 30 1959	Norwich City	L 0-4

F.A. Cup

Nov 15 1958	Exeter City (First Round)	W 3-2
Dec 6 1958	Kings Lynn (Second Round)	W 3-1
Jan 10 1959	Barnsley (Third Round)	W 2-0

1959-1960

Football League Division Three

Aug 25 1959	Wrexham	W 3-1
Aug 29 1959	Southampton	D 2-2
Sep 8 1959	Bury	D 1-1

Sep 12 1959	Shrewsbury Town	W 2-1
Sep 22 1959	Halifax Town	D 1-1
Sep 26 1959	Norwich City	L 3-4
Oct 6 1959	Colchester United	W 2-0
Oct 10 1959	Tranmere Rovers	W 2-1
Oct 24 1959	Accrington Stanley	W 3-0
Nov 21 1959	York City	L 1-2
Dec 19 1959	Barnsley	W 3-0
Dec 28 1959	Southend United	W 3-1
Jan 16 1960	Reading	D 2-2
Feb 6 1960	Port Vale	W 2-0
Feb 20 1960	Grimsby Town	L 0-2
Mar 5 1960	Bournemouth and Boscombe Athletic	W 1-0
Mar 8 1960	Chesterfield	W 3-0
Mar 19 1960	Coventry City	W 3-1
Apr 2 1960	Swindon Town	W 2-1
Apr 15 1960	Mansfield Town	D 1-1
Apr 16 1960	Queens Park Rangers	D 1-1
Apr 30 1960	Newport County	L 1-2
May 3 1960	Bradford City	W 4-0

F.A. Cup

| Nov 14 1959 | Ashford Town (First Round) | W 5-0 |

1960-1961

Football League Division Three

Aug 20 1960	Tranmere Rovers	W 4-1
Aug 23 1960	Watford	W 2-1
Sep 3 1960	Shrewsbury Town	W 4-0
Sep 6 1960	Torquay United	L 2-3
Sep 17 1960	Bury	L 1-5
Sep 27 1960	Queens Park Rangers	W 2-0
Oct 1 1960	Southend United	D 1-1
Oct 15 1960	Bradford City	D 2-2
Oct 29 1960	Newport County	L 2-4
Nov 12 1960	Grimsby Town	L 0-1
Dec 10 1960	Bristol City	W 2-0
Dec 23 1960	Swindon Town	W 2-1
Dec 31 1960	Halifax Town	W 2-0
Jan 21 1961	Walsall	W 3-1
Feb 11 1961	Chesterfield	D 2-2
Feb 25 1961	Coventry City	D 1-1
Mar 11 1961	Barnsley	D 0-0
Mar 25 1961	Colchester United	D 0-0
Apr 3 1961	Notts County	W 3-0

Apr 8 1961	Hull City	D 2-2
Apr 22 1961	Bournemouth and Boscombe Athletic	D 2-2
Apr 25 1961	Port Vale	D 0-0
May 2 1961	Reading	W 2-1

F.A. Cup

Nov 8 1960	Watford (First Round replay)	L 0-2

Football League Cup

Oct 25 1960	Sunderland (Second Round)	W 4-3
Nov 22 1960	Burnley (Third Round)	D 1-1

1961-1962

Football League Division Three

Aug 22 1961	Halifax Town	L 0-2
Aug 26 1961	Reading	L 1-2
Sep 9 1961	Southend United	D 0-0
Sep 19 1961	Coventry City	W 2-1
Sep 23 1961	Shrewsbury Town	W 4-0
Oct 7 1961	Swindon Town	W 1-0
Oct 10 1961	Bristol City	L 0-2
Oct 21 1961	Portsmouth	W 3-2
Nov 18 1961	Bournemouth and Boscombe Athletic	D 2-2
Dec 2 1961	Lincoln City	W 1-0
Dec 16 1961	Queens Park Rangers	L 1-4
Dec 26 1961	Bradford Park Avenue	W 2-0
Jan 13 1962	Newport County	W 3-1
Feb 2 1962	Notts County	L 0-1
Feb 17 1962	Peterborough United	W 2-0
Mar 3 1962	Torquay United	L 0-2
Mar 17 1962	Barnsley	D 1-1
Mar 30 1962	Watford	W 3-1
Apr 13 1962	Crystal Palace	W 4-2
Apr 20 1962	Port Vale	L 1-2
Apr 27 1962	Northampton Town	W 3-0
May 1 1962	Grimsby Town	L 0-2
May 3 1962	Hull City	L 0-2

F.A. Cup

Nov 4 1961	Oxford United (First Round)	W 3-0
Nov 28 1961	Aldershot (Second Round replay)	W 2-0
Jan 6 1962	Leyton Orient (Third Round)	D 1-1

1962-1963

Football League Division Four

Aug 21 1962	Gillingham	L 1-2
Aug 25 1962	Mansfield Town	L 1-3
Sep 8 1962	Exeter City	W 3-1
Sep 18 1962	Stockport County	W 2-1
Sep 22 1962	Rochdale	W 1-0
Sep 29 1962	Barrow	W 2-1
Oct 2 1962	Hartlepools United	W 4-0
Oct 13 1962	Southport	D 3-3
Oct 27 1962	Newport County	W 3-1
Nov 10 1962	Bradford City	W 5-2
Dec 8 1962	Oldham Athletic	W 2-1
Dec 15 1962	Doncaster Rovers	W 1-0
Dec 26 1962	Chester	W 2-1
Feb 23 1963	Darlington	L 1-3
Mar 9 1963	Aldershot	W 4-2
Mar 12 1963	Torquay United	D 2-2
Mar 23 1963	Oxford United	W 4-0
Apr 6 1963	Tranmere Rovers	W 4-0
Apr 15 1963	York City	W 2-1
Apr 20 1963	Lincoln City	W 3-2
Apr 30 1963	Crewe Alexandra	W 3-1
May 4 1963	Chesterfield	W 2-1
May 23 1963	Workington	W 4-3

Football League Cup

Sep 4 1962	Wrexham (First Round)	W 3-0
Sep 26 1962	Sheffield United (Second Round)	L 1-4

1963-1964

Football League Division Three (Southern Section)

Aug 24 1963	Notts County	W 4-1
Aug 27 1963	Bristol City	L 1-2
Sep 7 1963	Crystal Palace	W 2-1
Sep 21 1963	Reading	W 4-2
Oct 1 1963	Port Vale	L 1-2
Oct 5 1963	Coventry City	L 2-3
Oct 12 1963	Bristol Rovers	L 2-5
Oct 15 1963	Wrexham	W 9-0
Oct 26 1963	Millwall	W 3-1
Oct 29 1963	Mansfield Town	W 4-0

Nov 9 1963	Watford	L 1-2
Nov 23 1963	Peterborough United	W 2-0
Dec 21 1963	Crewe Alexandra	D 2-2
Jan 18 1964	Walsall	D 1-1
Feb 8 1964	Luton Town	L 2-6
Feb 29 1964	Queens Park Rangers	D 2-2
Mar 14 1964	Colchester United	W 3-1
Mar 28 1964	Southend United	W 3-0
Mar 30 1964	Shrewsbury Town	L 0-1
Apr 11 1964	Oldham Athletic	W 2-0
Apr 13 1964	Bournemouth and Boscombe Athletic	W 2-0
Apr 25 1964	Barnsley	D 1-1
Apr 28 1964	Hull City	L 1-3

F.A. Cup

Nov 16 1963	Margate (First Round)	D 2-2
Dec 17 1963	Gravesend and Northfleet (Second Round)	W 1-0
Jan 4 1964	Middlesbrough (Third Round)	W 2-1
Jan 28 1964	Oxford United (Fourth Round replay)	L 1-2

Football League Cup

| Sep 23 1963 | Reading (First Round replay) | W 2-0 |
| Sep 25 1963 | Bournemouth and Boscombe Athletic (Second Round) | D 0-0 |

1964-1965

Football League Division Three

Aug 22 1964	Luton Town	D 2-2
Aug 31 1964	Mansfield Town	W 1-0
Sep 5 1964	Port Vale	W 4-0
Sep 15 1964	Grimsby Town	W 2-0
Sep 19 1964	Gillingham	W 2-0
2Sep 6 1964	Bristol Rovers	D 1-1
Oct 6 1964	Peterborough United	W 3-1
Oct 17 1964	Shrewsbury Town	W 2-0
Oct 20 1964	Exeter City	W 2-1
Oct 27 1964	Hull City	L 1-3
Oct 31 1964	Southend United	W 2-1
Nov 28 1964	Watford	W 5-1
Dec 19 1964	Carlisle United	W 6-1
Dec 26 1964	Bristol City	W 2-1
Jan 16 1965	Colchester United	W 1-0
Feb 13 1965	Oldham Athletic	D 2-2

Feb 20 1965	Queens Park Rangers	W 5-2
Mar 20 1965	Barnsley	W 1-0
Apr 3 1965	Walsall	D 0-0
Apr 7 1965	Workington	W 3-0
Apr 16 1965	Bournemouth and Boscombe Athletic	W 2-1
Apr 17 1965	Reading	W 2-1
Apr 27 1965	Scunthorpe United	W 4-0

F.A. Cup

| Dec 5 1964 | Notts County (Second Round) | W 4-0 |
| Jan 12 1965 | Burnley (Third Round replay) | L 0-2 |

Football League Cup

| Sep 3 1964 | Southend United (First Round) | L 0-2 |

1965-1966

Football League Division Three

Aug 21 1965	Queens Park Rangers	W 6-1
Sep 4 1965	York City	L 0-1
Sep 14 1965	Shrewsbury Town	W 4-0
Sep 18 1965	Swansea Town	W 2-0
Oct 2 1965	Workington	L 0-1
Oct 9 1965	Scunthorpe United	L 0-1
Oct 23 1965	Oldham Athletic	D 0-0
Nov 6 1965	Millwall	L 1-2
Nov 20 1965	Exeter City	L 1-2
Nov 23 1965	Grimsby Town	W 3-2
Jan 8 1966	Peterborough United	W 1-0
Feb 5 1966	Bristol Rovers	L 0-5
Feb 26 1966	Oxford United	W 5-1
Mar 1 1966	Southend United	W 2-0
Mar 5 1966	Swindon Town	L 0-1
Mar 19 1966	Walsall	D 2-2
Apr 9 1966	Hull City	L 2-4
Apr 11 1966	Brighton and Hove Albion	W 2-0
Apr 23 1966	Reading	D 1-1
May 7 1966	Mansfield Town	L 0-3
May 10 1966	Watford	D 1-1
May 17 1966	Bournemouth and Boscombe Athletic	W 1-0
May 28 1966	Gillingham	L 0-2

F.A. Cup

| Nov 13 1965 | Yeovil Town (First Round) | W 2-1 |

Football League Cup

Sep 30 1965	Workington (First Round replay)	L 1-2

1966-1967

Football League Division Four

Aug 27 1966	Luton Town	W 1-0
Sep 10 1966	Wrexham	D 1-1
Sep 24 1966	Tranmere Rovers	D 1-1
Sep 27 1966	Lincoln City	D 2-2
Oct 11 1966	Aldershot	W 1-0
Oct 15 1966	Stockport County	W 2-1
Oct 18 1966	Halifax Town	W 1-0
Oct 29 1966	Southport	W 2-1
Nov 12 1966	Chester	W 4-0
Dec 10 1966	Barrow	L 0-3
Dec 17 1966	Barnsley	W 3-1
Dec 27 1966	Hartlepools United	D 2-2
Jan 21 1967	Southend United	D 1-1
Feb 11 1967	Bradford City	W 2-0
Feb 18 1967	York City	D 1-1
Feb 25 1967	Chesterfield	W 1-0
Mar 18 1967	Rochdale	W 4-0
Mar 27 1967	Newport County	D 1-1
Apr 1 1967	Notts County	W 1-0
Apr 11 1967	Exeter City	W 3-1
Apr 15 1967	Bradford Park Avenue	D 1-1
Apr 29 1967	Crewe Alexandra	L 0-2
May 13 1967	Port Vale	W 2-0

F.A. Cup

Nov 26 1966	Chelmsford City (First Round)	W 1-0
Jan 10 1967	Leyton Orient (Third Round replay)	W 3-1

Football League Cup

Aug 24 1966	Millwall (First Round0	D 0-0
Sep 13 1966	Ipswich Town (Second Round)	L 2-4

1967-1968

Football League Division Four

Aug 26 1967	Newport County	W 3-1
Sep 9 1967	Rochdale	W 4-0
Sep 16 1967	Halifax Town	D 0-0
Sep 26 1967	Swansea Town	W 2-1
Sep 30 1967	Doncaster Rovers	W 4-2
Oct 14 1967	Notts County	W 2-1
Oct 24 1967	Wrexham	D 0-0
Oct 28 1967	Chester	W 3-1
Nov 11 1967	Exeter City	W 5-1
Nov 14 1967	York City	W 3-1
Nov 25 1967	Aldershot	D 1-1
Dec 16 1967	Hartlepools United	L 0-1
Dec 26 1967	Southend United	L 1-2
Jan 6 1968	Barnsley	L 0-2
Jan 27 1968	Bradford City	L 0-1
Feb 3 1968	Bradford Park Avenue	W 2-1
Feb 17 1968	Luton Town	L 0-2
Feb 24 1968	Darlington	W 2-0
Mar 16 1968	Port Vale	W 3-1
Mar 30 1968	Chesterfield	D 1-1
Apr 13 1968	Crewe Alexandra	W 2-0
Apr 23 1968	Lincoln City	L 1-3
Apr 27 1968	Workington	W 2-0

F.A. Cup

| Dec 14 1967 | Guildford City (First Round) | D 2-2 |

1968-1969

Football League Division Four

Aug 10 1968	Colchester United	W 4-0
Aug 24 1968	Port Vale	W 3-1
Aug 26 1968	Rochdale	D 1-1
Sep 7 1968	Chesterfield	W 1-0
Sep 21 1968	York City	W 5-1
Oct 5 1968	Newport County	D 1-1
Oct 19 1968	Wrexham	D 1-1
Nov 2 1968	Aldershot	L 2-4
Nov 4 1968	Darlington	L 0-1
Nov 30 1968	Halifax Town	D 1-1
Dec 14 1968	Swansea Town	W 2-1
Jan 4 1969	Workington	L 0-3
Jan 18 1969	Lincoln City	D 2-2
Feb 22 1969	Grimsby Town	W 4-2
Mar 8 1969	Scunthorpe United	W 2-1
Mar 10 1969	Southend United	D 1-1

Mar 22 1969	Exeter City	L 0-1
Mar 26 1969	Notts County	D 0-0
Apr 14 1969	Doncaster Rovers	W 1-0
Apr 19 1969	Peterborough United	W 2-0
Apr 21 1969	Bradford Park Avenue	W 3-0
Apr 30 1969	Chester	W 2-1
May 5 1969	Bradford City	W 2-1

F.A. Cup

| Nov 16 1968 | Woking (First Round) | W 2-0 |

Football League Cup

| Sep 4 1968 | Hull City (Second Round) | W 3-0 |
| Sep 24 1968 | Norwich City (Third Round) | L 0-2 |

1969-1970

Football League Division Four

Aug 16 1969	Notts County	W 1-0
Aug 30 1969	Darlington	D 1-1
Sep 13 1969	Swansea Town	D 2-2
Sep 15 1969	Southend United	W 3-1
Sep 27 1969	Wrexham	D 0-0
Sep 29 1969	Lincoln City	W 2-1
Oct 11 1969	Scunthorpe United	W 3-0
Oct 18 1969	Oldham Athletic	D 1-1
Nov 1 1969	Peterborough United	W 5-2
Nov 24 1969	Grimsby Town	W 3-0
Dec 20 1969	Newport County	W 1-0
Dec 26 1969	Crewe Alexandra	D 1-1
Jan 10 1970	Bradford Park Avenue	D 1-1
Jan 24 1970	Port Vale	W 1-0
Jan 31 1970	Workington	W 1-0
Feb 21 1970	Chesterfield	L 0-1
Feb 23 1970	Hartlepool	W 3-0
Mar 7 1970	Northampton Town	W 1-0
Mar 9 1970	York City	D 0-0
Mar 21 1970	Aldershot	D 0-0
Mar 27 1970	Exeter City	W 2-0
Apr 4 1970	Chester	W 2-0
Apr 18 1970	Colchester United	W 2-0

F.A. Cup

| Nov 15 1969 | Plymouth Argyle (First Round) | D 0-0 |

Football League Cup

18 Aug 1969   Southend United (First Round replay)   D 0-0

1970-71

Football League Division Four

Aug 15 1970	Chester	L 1-2
Aug 29 1970	Southport	L 0-1
Sep 12 1970	Peterborough United	D 1-1
Sep 26 1970	Darlington	W 1-0
Oct 10 1970	Bournemouth and Boscombe Athletic	L 1-2
Oct 19 1970	Aldershot	L 2-3
Oct 31 1970	Exeter City	W 5-0
Nov 9 1970	York City	W 6-4
Nov 14 1970	Grimsby Town	W 2-0
Dec 5 1970	Barrow	W 2-1
Dec 19 1970	Lincoln City	W 2-1
Jan 9 1971	Stockport County	W 3-0
Feb 23 1971	Hartlepool	W 1-0
Mar 6 1971	Southend United	W 4-2
Mar 8 1971	Crewe Alexandra	W 3-1
Mar 20 1971	Newport County	L 0-3
Mar 27 1971	Oldham Athletic	D 1-1
Mar 29 1971	Colchester United	W 1-0
Apr 9 1971	Northampton Town	W 3-0
Apr 10 1971	Scunthorpe United	L 0-1
Apr 24 1971	Notts County	D 2-2
Apr 26 1971	Cambridge United	L 1-2
May 7 1971	Workington	W 3-0

F.A. Cup

Nov 21 1970	Gillingham (First Round)	W 2-1
Dec 12 1970	Walsall (Second Round)	W 1-0

1971-1972

Football League Division Four

Aug 21 1971	Aldershot	D 1-1
Aug 30 1971	Barrow	W 4-0
Sep 4 1971	Hartlepool	W 6-0
Sep 18 1971	Peterborough United	W 5-1
Sep 27 1971	Stockport County	W 2-0

Oct 2 1971	Northampton Town	W 6-1
Oct 16 1971	Bury	W 2-0
Oct 23 1971	Southend United	L 1-2
Nov 6 1971	Newport County	W 3-1
Nov 27 1971	Gillingham	L 1-3
Dec 11 1971	Southport	W 1-0
Dec 27 1971	Crewe Alexandra	W 1-0
Jan 8 1972	Darlington	W 6-2
Jan 29 1972	Reading	L 1-2
Feb 19 1972	Scunthorpe United	L 0-3
Mar 4 1972	Colchester United	L 0-2
Mar 13 1972	Lincoln City	W 2-0
Mar 25 1972	Grimsby Town	W 2-0
Mar 27 1972	Workington	W 2-0
Mar 31 1972	Chester	D 1-1
Apr 8 1972	Cambridge United	W 2-1
Apr 17 1972	Doncaster Rovers	W 2-1
Apr 22 1972	Exeter City	W 1-0

F.A. Cup

| Nov 22 1971 | Swansea City (First Round replay) | L 2-3 |

1972-1973

Football League Division Three

Aug 12 1972	Halifax Town	L 0-1
Aug 26 1972	Blackburn Rovers	W 4-0
Aug 28 1972	Bolton Wanderers	W 2-1
Sep 9 1972	Swansea City	L 0-2
Sep 23 1972	AFC Bournemouth	D 1-1
Sep 25 1972	Bristol Rovers	W 2-1
Oct 9 1972	Tranmere Rovers	W 2-0
Oct 14 1972	Walsall	W 2-0
Oct 28 1972	Rochdale	W 1-0
Nov 11 1972	Chesterfield	W 3-1
Nov 25 1972	York City	W 2-0
Dec 23 1972	Wrexham	W 1-0
Dec 30 1972	Oldham Athletic	D 1-1
Jan 13 1973	Rotherham United	D 1-1
Jan 20 1973	Plymouth Argyle	L 0-2
Feb 10 1973	Port Vale	W 5-0
Feb 24 1973	Grimsby Town	L 0-1
Feb 26 1973	Charlton Athletic	W 1-0
Mar 3 1973	Scunthorpe United	W 1-0
Mar 17 1973	Southend United	L 1-2
Mar 19 1973	Watford	D 1-1

| Apr 7 1973 | Shrewsbury Town | L 1-2 |
| Apr 20 1973 | Notts County | D 1-1 |

Football League Cup

| Aug 16 1972 | Cambridge United (First Round) | W 1-0 |

1973-1974

Football League Division Four

Sep 1 1973	Exeter City	L 0-1
Sep 10 1973	Torquay United	D 0-0
Sep 15 1973	Doncaster Rovers	W 2-0
Sep 17 1973	Reading	L 0-1
Sep 29 1973	Barnsley	W 5-1
Oct 13 1973	Peterborough United	L 0-1
Oct 20 1973	Rotherham United	D 1-1
Nov 3 1973	Mansfield Town	W 4-1
Nov 17 1973	Chester	W 3-0
Dec 1 1973	Gillingham	L 0-3
Dec 15 1973	Darlington	D 0-0
Dec 26 1973	Newport County	D 1-1
Jan 5 1974	Swansea City	L 0-2
Jan 19 1974	Hartlepool	L 1-2
Feb 9 1974	Bury	L 1-2
Feb 23 1974	Lincoln City	W 2-1
Mar 9 1974	Scunthorpe United	W 2-1
Mar 18 1974	Northampton Town	W 3-1
Mar 23 1974	Workington	D 1-1
Apr 1 1974	Crewe Alexandra	W 3-0
Apr 6 1974	Stockport County	D 0-0
Apr 16 1974	Colchester United	D 0-0
Apr 20 1974	Bradford City	W 2-0

Football League Cup

| Aug 28 1973 | Orient (First Round) | L 1-2 |

1974-1975

Football League Division Four

Aug 17 1974	Northampton Town	W 1-0
Aug 31 1974	Swansea City	W 1-0
Sep 14 1974	Cambridge United	W 1-0
Sep 16 1974	Rotherham United	L 3-4

Sep 28 1974	Crewe Alexandra	W 1-0
Oct 12 1974	Lincoln City	D 1-1
Oct 26 1974	Torquay United	W 3-1
Nov 4 1974	Bradford City	D 0-0
Nov 9 1974	Mansfield Town	L 2-3
Dec 7 1974	Darlington	W 3-0
Dec 21 1974	Scunthorpe United	W 2-0
Dec 28 1974	Exeter City	W 2-0
Jan 18 1975	Workington	D 2-2
Jan 25 1975	Reading	W 1-0
Feb 8 1975	Barnsley	W 3-0
Feb 22 1975	Hartlepool	W 1-0
Mar 8 1975	Rochdale	W 3-0
Mar 22 1975	Chester	D 1-1
Apr 1 1975	Newport County	D 0-0
Apr 7 1975	Stockport County	W 3-0
Apr 12 1975	Doncaster Rovers	D 1-1
Apr 21 1975	Southport	W 1-0
Apr 26 1975	Shrewsbury Town	W 2-1

Football League Cup

| Aug 21 1974 | Aldershot (First Round) | W 3-0 |

1975-1976

Football League Division Four

Aug 23 1975	Hartlepool	D 1-1
Sep 6 1975	Barnsley	W 1-0
Sep 20 1975	Stockport County	W 2-1
Oct 4 1975	Newport County	L 1-3
Oct 18 1975	Southport	W 1-0
Nov 1 1975	Scunthorpe United	W 5-2
Nov 3 1975	Workington	W 4-0
Nov 15 1975	Watford	W 1-0
Dec 6 1975	Rochdale	W 3-0
Dec 20 1975	Darlington	W 3-0
Dec 27 1975	Reading	D 2-2
Jan 10 1976	Torquay United	D 1-1
Jan 24 1976	Doncaster Rovers	L 0-1
Jan 31 1976	Northampton Town	W 2-1
Feb 14 1976	Tranmere Rovers	L 0-1
Feb 23 1976	AFC Bournemouth	L 1-2
Feb 28 1976	Cambridge United	D 0-0
Mar 13 1976	Lincoln City	W 1-0
Mar 20 1976	Crewe Alexandra	D 0-0
Apr 3 1976	Bradford City	D 2-2

Apr 5 1976	Huddersfield Town	D 0-0
Apr 16 1976	Swansea City	W 1-0
Apr 17 1976	Exeter City	W 5-1

F.A. Cup

| Nov 22 1975 | Northampton Town (First Round) | W 2-0 |
| Jan 3 1976 | Bolton Wanderers (Third Round) | D 0-0 |

Football League Cup

| Aug 19 1975 | Brighton and Hove Albion (First Round - First Leg) | W 2-1 |

1976-77

Football League Division Four

Aug 21 1976	Barnsley	L 0-1
Sep 4 1976	Doncaster Rovers	D 2-2
Sep 18 1976	Southport	W 3-0
Oct 9 1976	Newport County	D 1-1
Oct 23 1976	Darlington	L 0-3
Oct 25 1976	Workington	W 5-0
Nov 6 1976	AFC Bournemouth	W 3-2
Nov 27 1976	Cambridge United	L 0-2
Jan 3 1977	Colchester United	L 1-4
Jan 15 1977	Stockport County	W 4-0
Jan 29 1977	Halifax Town	W 2-1
Feb 5 1977	Huddersfield Town	L 1-3
Feb 19 1977	Aldershot	L 0-1
Feb 22 1977	Rochdale	W 3-2
Mar 5 1977	Torquay United	W 3-2
Mar 12 1977	Bradford City	W 4-0
Mar 23 1977	Watford	W 3-0
Mar 26 1977	Swansea City	W 4-0
Apr 8 1977	Southend United	W 1-0
Apr 12 1977	Exeter City	W 1-0
Apr 23 1977	Hartlepool	W 3-1
May 2 1977	Crewe Alexandra	D 0-0
May 7 1977	Scunthorpe United	W 4-2

F.A. Cup

| Nov 20 1976 | Chesham United (First Round) | W 2-0 |

Football League Cup

Aug 17 1976   Watford (First Round -Second Leg)   L 0-2

1977-78

Football League Division Four

Aug 20 1977	Northampton Town	W 3-0
Aug 22 1977	Wimbledon	W 4-1
Aug 27 1977	Reading	D 1-1
Sep 10 1977	AFC Bournemouth	D 1-1
Sep 24 1977	Scunthorpe United	W 2-0
Oct 1 1977	Halifax Town	W 4-1
Oct 3 1977	Watford	L 0-3
Oct 15 1977	Southport	D 0-0
Oct 29 1977	Southend United	W 1-0
Nov 5 1977	York City	W 1-0
Nov 19 1977	Swansea City	L 0-2
Dec 10 1977	Grimsby Town	W 3-1
Dec 27 1977	Newport County	D 3-3
Jan 2 1978	Huddersfield Town	D 1-1
Jan 28 1978	Crewe Alexandra	W 5-1
Mar 4 1978	Torquay United	W 3-0
Mar 6 1978	Rochdale	W 4-0
Mar 18 1978	Hartlepool	W 2-0
Mar 27 1978	Aldershot	W 2-0
Apr 3 1978	Stockport County	W 4-0
Apr 8 1978	Barnsley	W 2-0
Apr 18 1978	Doncaster Rovers	D 2-2
Apr 22 1978	Darlington	W 2-0

F.A. Cup

Nov 26 1977   Folkestone and Shepway (First Round)   W 2-0

Football League Cup

Aug 13 1977   Crystal Palace (First Round - First Leg)   W 2-1

1978-1979

Football League Division Three

Aug 21 1978	Colchester United	W 1-0
Aug 26 1978	Chesterfield	L 0-3
Sep 9 1978	Hull City	W 1-0
Sep 23 1978	Gillingham	L 0-2
Sep 25 1978	Lincoln City	W 2-1

Oct 7 1978	Bury	L 0-1
Oct 21 1978	Tranmere Rovers	W 2-0
Nov 4 1978	Oxford United	W 3-0
Nov 11 1978	Exeter City	D 0-0
Dec 2 1978	Walsall	W 1-0
Dec 26 1978	Plymouth Argyle	W 2-1
Dec 30 1978	Carlisle United	D 0-0
Jan 20 1979	Peterborough United	D 0-0
Feb 10 1979	Swansea City	W 1-0
Feb 24 1979	Watford	D 3-3
Mar 10 1979	Chester	W 6-0
Mar 26 1979	Shrewsbury Town	L 2-3
Mar 31 1979	Blackpool	W 3-2
Apr 13 1979	Southend United	W 3-0
Apr 17 1979	Sheffield Wednesday	W 2-1
Apr 23 1979	Rotherham United	W 1-0
Apr 28 1979	Mansfield Town	W 1-0
May 8 1979	Swindon Town	L 1-2

Football League Cup

Aug 15 1978	Watford (First Round - Second Leg)	L 1-3

1979-1980

Football League Division Three

Sep 1 1979	Chesterfield	W 3-1
Sep 15 1979	Grimsby Town	W 1-0
Sep 17 1979	Exeter City	L 0-2
Sep 29 1979	Southend United	W 2-0
Oct 6 1979	Barnsley	W 3-1
Oct 20 1979	Blackburn Rovers	W 2-0
Oct 22 1979	Sheffield United	L 1-2
Nov 3 1979	Reading	D 2-2
Nov 10 1979	Colchester United	W 1-0
Dec 8 1979	Hull City	W 7-2
Dec 15 1979	Oxford United	D 1-1
Dec 26 1979	Chester	D 2-2
Dec 29 1979	Swindon Town	L 1-3
Jan 5 1980	Gillingham	L 0-2
Jan 19 1980	Sheffield Wednesday	D 2-2
Feb 9 1980	Wimbledon	L 0-1
Feb 23 1980	Blackpool	W 2-1
Mar 8 1980	Plymouth Argyle	D 0-0
Mar 29 1980	Rotherham United	L 0-1
Apr 7 1980	Mansfield Town	W 2-0
Apr 8 1980	Bury	D 0-0

| Apr 19 1980 | Carlisle United | L 0-3 |
| May 3 1980 | Millwall | W 1-0 |

Football League Cup

| Aug 21 1979 | Southend United (First Round - Second Leg) | L 1-4 |

1980-81

Football League Division Three

Aug 18 1980	Millwall	W 1-0
Aug 23 1980	Reading	L 1-2
Sep 13 1980	Fulham	L 1-3
Sep 15 1980	Barnsley	D 1-1
Sep 27 1980	Hull City	D 2-2
Oct 4 1980	Newport County	L 0-1
Oct 18 1980	Chester	L 0-1
Oct 20 1980	Gillingham	D 3-3
Nov 1 1980	Oxford United	W 3-0
Nov 3 1980	Exeter City	L 0-1
Nov 15 1980	Charlton Athletic	L 0-1
Dec 6 1980	Swindon Town	D 1-1
Dec 26 1980	Colchester United	W 2-1
Jan 3 1981	Burnley	D 0-0
Jan 17 1981	Huddersfield Town	D 0-0
Jan 24 1981	Walsall	W 4-0
Feb 14 1981	Portsmouth	D 2-2
Feb 28 1981	Blackpool	W 2-0
Mar 14 1981	Carlisle United	D 1-1
Mar 28 1981	Plymouth Argyle	L 0-1
Apr 11 1981	Chesterfield	W 3-2
Apr 18 1981	Sheffield United	D 1-1
Apr 25 1981	Rotherham United	W 2-1

F.A. Cup

| Nov 22 1980 | Addlestone and Weybridge Town (First Round)* | D 2-2 |
| Nov 25 1980 | Addlestone and Weybridge Town (First Round replay) | W 2-0 |

*Played at Griffin Park, Addlestone's ground unsuitable.

Football League Cup

| Aug 9 1980 | Charlton Athletic (First Round - First Leg) | W 3-1 |

1981-82

Football League Division Three

Sep 5 1981	Walsall	D 0-0
Sep 19 1981	Plymouth Argyle	D 0-0
Sep 21 1981	Gillingham	L 0-1
Oct 3 1981	Carlisle United	L 1-2
Oct 17 1981	Lincoln City	W 3-1
Oct 19 1981	Southend United	L 0-1
Oct 31 1981	Burnley	D 0-0
Nov 7 1981	Bristol City	L 0-1
Nov 28 1981	Chester	W 1-0
Jan 2 1982	Huddersfield Town	L 0-1
Jan 23 1982	Fulham	L 0-1
Feb 6 1982	Portsmouth	D 2-2
Feb 20 1982	Newport County	W 2-0
Feb 27 1982	Exeter City	W 2-0
Mar 13 1982	Chesterfield	W 2-0
Mar 22 1982	Bristol Rovers	W 1-0
Apr 3 1982	Oxford United	L 1-2
Apr 9 1982	Millwall	W 4-1
Apr 17 1982	Preston North End	D 0-0
Apr 19 1982	Swindon Town	W 4-2
Apr 26 1982	Wimbledon	L 2-3
May 1 1982	Doncaster Rovers	D 2-2
May 15 1982	Reading	L 1-2

F.A. Cup

Nov 21 1981	Exeter City (First Round)	W 2-0
Dec 16 1981	Colchester United (Second Round)	D 1-1

Football League Cup

Sep 15 1981	Oxford United (First Round - Second Leg)	L 0-2

1982-83

Football League Division Three

Aug 28 1982	Bristol Rovers	W 5-1
Sep 11 1982	Southend United	W 4-2
Sep 25 1982	Millwall	D 1-1
Sep 28 1982	Newport County	W 2-0
Oct 9 1982	Chesterfield	W 4-2
Oct 23 1982	Lincoln City	W 2-0

Nov 2 1982	Preston North End	W 3-1
Nov 6 1982	Bradford City	L 0-2
Dec 4 1982	Wrexham	W 4-1
Dec 18 1982	Exeter City	W 4-0
Dec 28 1982	Gillingham	D 1-1
Jan 3 1983	Cardiff City	L 1-3
Jan 8 1983	Wigan Athletic	L 1-3
Jan 22 1983	Orient	W 5-2
Feb 12 1983	Reading	L 1-2
Feb 26 1983	Doncaster Rovers	W 1-0
Mar 11 1983	Plymouth Argyle	W 2-0
Mar 22 1983	Oxford United	D 1-1
Mar 26 1983	Huddersfield Town	W 1-0
Apr 1 1983	Portsmouth	D 1-1
Apr 16 1983	Walsall	L 2-3
Apr 30 1983	Sheffield United	W 2-1
May 14 1983	AFC Bournemouth	W 2-1

F.A. Cup

| Nov 20 1982 | Windsor and Eton (First Round)* | W 7-0 |
| Dec 14 1982 | Swindon Town (Second Round replay) | L 1-3 |

*Played at Griffin Park, Windsor & Eton's ground unsuitable.

Milk Cup

Sep 14 1982	Wimbledon (First Round - Second Leg)	W 2-0
Oct 5 1982	Blackburn Rovers (Second Round - First Leg)	W 3-2
Nov 9 1982	Swansea City (Third Round)	D 1-1

Football League Trophy

| Aug 14 1982 | Crystal Palace | D 2-2 |

1983-84

Canon League Division Three

Aug 27 1983	Millwall	D 2-2
Sep 10 1983	Lincoln City	W 3-0
Sep 24 1983	Burnley	D 0-0
Oct 15 1983	Hull City	D 1-1
Oct 18 1983	Port Vale	W 3-1
Oct 29 1983	AFC Bournemouth	D 1-1
Nov 5 1983	Plymouth Argyle	D 2-2
Nov 26 1983	Bradford City	L 1-4
Dec 24 1983	Wimbledon	L 3-4

Dec 31 1983	Newport County	W 2-0
Jan 21 1984	Wigan Athletic	L 0-1
Feb 4 1984	Gillingham	L 2-3
Feb 14 1984	Southend United	D 0-0
Feb 25 1984	Sheffield United	L 1-3
Mar 10 1984	Orient	D 1-1
Mar 17 1984	Oxford United	L 1-2
Mar 20 1984	Rotherham United	W 2-1
Mar 31 1984	Bristol Rovers	D 2-2
Apr 3 1984	Preston North End	W 4-1
Apr 14 1984	Bolton Wanderers	W 3-0
Apr 20 1984	Exeter City	W 3-0
May 5 1984	Scunthorpe United	W 3-0
May 12 1984	Walsall	D 1-1

F.A. Cup

| Nov 22 1983 | Dagenham (First Round replay) | W 2-1 |
| Dec 10 1983 | Wimbledon (Second Round) | W 3-2 |

Milk Cup

| Aug 30 1983 | Charlton Athletic (First Round - First Leg) | W 3-0 |
| Oct 5 1983 | Liverpool (Second Round - First Leg) | L 1-4 |

Associate Members Cup

| Feb 21 1984 | Orient (First Round) | W 3-2 |

1984-85

Canon League Division Three

Aug 25 1984	Orient	L 0-1
Sep 8 1984	Wigan Athletic	W 2-0
Sep 22 1984	Swansea City	W 3-0
Oct 2 1984	Doncaster Rovers	D 1-1
Oct 6 1984	Bradford City	L 0-1
Oct 20 1984	Gillingham	W 5-2
Oct 27 1984	York City	W 2-1
Nov 10 1984	Lincoln City	D 2-2
Dec 1 1984	Bolton Wanderers	W 2-1
Dec 26 1984	Bristol Rovers	L 0-3
Dec 29 1984	Reading	W 2-1
Jan 26 1985	Newport County	L 2-5
Feb 2 1985	Cambridge United	W 2-0
Feb 23 1985	Bristol City	L 1-2
Mar 5 1985	Burnley	W 2-1

Mar 27 1985	Walsall	W 3-1
Mar 30 1985	Derby County	D 1-1
Apr 8 1985	Plymouth Argyle	W 3-1
Apr 20 1985	AFC Bournemouth	D 0-0
Apr 23 1985	Rotherham United	W 3-0
May 4 1985	Preston North End	W 3-1
May 11 1985	Hull City	W 2-1
May 19 1985	Millwall	D 1-1

F.A. Cup

| Nov 17 1984 | Bishop's Stortford (First Round) | W 4-0 |
| Dec 8 1984 | Northampton Town (Second Round) | D 2-2 |

Milk Cup

| Aug 28 1984 | Cambridge United (First Round - First Leg) | W 2-0 |
| Oct 9 1984 | Leicester City (Second Round - Second Leg) | L 0-2 |

Freight Rover Trophy

Feb 26 1985	Reading (First Round)	W 2-0
Mar 19 1985	Cambridge United (Second Round)	W 1-0
May 17 1985	Newport County (Southern Area Final)	W 6-0

1985-86

Canon League Division Three

Aug 17 1985	Wolverhampton Wanderers	W 2-1
Aug 26 1985	AFC Bournemouth	W 1-0
Sep 7 1985	Plymouth Argyle	D 1-1
Sep 17 1985	Reading	L 1-2
Sep 28 1985	Rotherham United	D 1-1
Oct 5 1985	Swansea City	W 1-0
Oct 19 1985	Newport County	D 0-0
Nov 2 1985	Cardiff City	W 3-0
Nov 6 1985	Derby County	D 3-3
Nov 23 1985	Chesterfield	W 1-0
Dec 14 1985	Bury	W 1-0
Dec 22 1985	Bristol Rovers	W 1-0
Jan 11 1986	Wigan Athletic	L 1-3
Jan 21 1986	Notts County	D 1-1
Jan 24 1986	Doncaster Rovers	L 1-3
Feb 4 1986	Walsall	L 1-3
Mar 14 1986	Bolton Wanderers	D 1-1

Mar 22 1986	Blackpool	D 1-1
Mar 31 1986	Gillingham	L 1-2
Apr 13 1986	Bristol City	L 1-2
Apr 22 1986	Lincoln City	L 0-1
Apr 26 1986	York City	D 3-3
May 5 1986	Darlington	W 2-1

F.A. Cup

| Nov 16 1985 | Bristol Rovers (First Round) | L 1-3 |

Milk Cup

| Sep 3 1985 | Cambridge United (First Round - Second Leg) | W 2-0 |
| Sep 25 1985 | Sheffield Wednesday (Second Round - First Leg) | D 2-2 |

Freight Rover Trophy

| Jan 15 1986 | Derby County (First Round) | D 0-0 |

1986-1987

Today League Division Three

Aug 23 1986	AFC Bournemouth	D 1-1
Sep 6 1986	Port Vale	L 0-2
Sep 20 1986	Darlington	W 5-3
Sep 30 1986	Bury	L 0-2
Oct 4 1986	Newport County	W 2-0
Oct 18 1986	York City	W 3-1
Nov 1 1986	Bolton Wanderers	L 1-2
Nov 4 1986	Notts County	W 1-0
Nov 22 1986	Blackpool	D 1-1
Dec 21 1986	Middlesbrough	L 0-1
Dec 28 1986	Bristol Rovers	L 1-2
Jan 1 1987	Chesterfield	D 2-2
Feb 1 1987	Fulham	D 3-3
Feb 7 1987	Carlisle United	W 3-1
Feb 21 1987	Gillingham	W 3-2
Mar 7 1987	Walsall	L 0-1
Mar 17 1987	Bristol City	D 1-1
Mar 21 1987	Mansfield Town	W 3-1
Apr 4 1987	Chester City	W 3-1
Apr 14 1987	Doncaster Rovers	D 1-1
Apr 20 1987	Swindon Town	D 1-1
May 2 1987	Rotherham United	W 2-0

| May 9 1987 | Wigan Athletic | L 2-3 |

F.A. Cup

| Dec 6 1986 | Bristol Rovers (Second Round replay) | W 2-0 |

Littlewoods Cup

| Sep 2 1986 | Southend United (First Round - Second Leg) | L 2-3 |

Freight Rover Trophy

| Jan 6 1987 | Swindon Town (First Round) | W 4-2 |
| Jan 26 1987 | Walsall (Second Round) | W 4-2 |

1987-1988

Barclays League Division Three

Aug 15 1987	Sunderland	L 0-1
Aug 29 1987	Bristol City	L 0-2
Sep 5 1987	Rotherham United	D 1-1
Sep 15 1987	Chesterfield	W 2-0
Sep 19 1987	Blackpool	W 2-1
Oct 3 1987	Port Vale	W 1-0
Oct 17 1987	Walsall	D 0-0
Oct 20 1987	Chester City	D 1-1
Oct 31 1987	Bristol Rovers	D 1-1
Nov 21 1987	Wigan Athletic	W 2-1
Dec 12 1987	Mansfield Town	D 2-2
Dec 26 1987	Aldershot	W 3-0
Jan 2 1988	Southend United	W 1-0
Jan 9 1988	Northampton Town	L 0-1
Feb 14 1988	Fulham	W 3-1
Feb 23 1988	Grimsby Town	L 0-2
Mar 1 1988	Preston North End	W 2-0
Mar 12 1988	Bury	L 0-3
Mar 26 1988	Brighton and Hove Albion	D 1-1
Apr 2 1988	Notts County	W 1-0
Apr 9 1988	Gillingham	D 2-2
Apr 30 1988	Doncaster Rovers	D 1-1
May 7 1988	York City	L 1-2

F.A. Cup

| Nov 14 1987 | Brighton and Hove Albion (First Round) | L 0-2 |

Littlewoods Cup

Aug 18 1987	Southend United (First Round - First Leg)	W 2-1

Sherpa Van Trophy

Nov 24 1987	Notts County (Preliminary Round)	W 3-2

1988-1989

Barclays League Division Three

Aug 27 1988	Huddersfield Town	W 1-0
Sep 10 1988	Wigan Athletic	D 1-1
Sep 24 1988	Sheffield United	L 1-4
Oct 1 1988	Gillingham	W 1-0
Oct 9 1988	Southend United	W 4-0
Oct 22 1988	Preston North End	L 0-2
Oct 29 1988	Port Vale	W 2-1
Nov 8 1988	Notts County	W 2-1
Dec 3 1988	Bolton Wanderers	W 3-0
Dec 26 1988	Blackpool	W 1-0
Dec 31 1988	Wolverhampton Wanderers	D 2-2
Jan 14 1989	Northampton Town	W 2-0
Feb 11 1989	Chester City	L 0-1
Feb 25 1989	Bury	D 2-2
Feb 28 1989	Chesterfield	W 1-0
Mar 11 1989	Reading	W 3-2
Mar 24 1989	Fulham	L 0-1
Apr 1 1989	Aldershot	W 2-1
Apr 4 1989	Bristol City	W 3-0
Apr 15 1989	Bristol Rovers	W 2-1
Apr 29 1989	Mansfield Town	W 1-0
May 9 1989	Swansea City	D 1-1
May 13 1989	Cardiff City	D 1-1

F.A. Cup

Nov 19 1988	Halesowen Town (First Round)	W 2-0
Dec 14 1988	Peterborough United (Second Round replay)	W 3-2
Jan 10 1989	Walsall (Third Round replay)	W 1-0
Jan 28 1989	Manchester City (Fourth Round)	W 3-1

Littlewoods Cup

Sep 6 1988	Fulham (First Round - Second Leg)	W 1-0

| Oct 12 1988 | Blackburn Rovers (Second Round - Second Leg) | W 4-3 |

Sherpa Van Trophy

Nov 29 1988	Gillingham (Preliminary Round)	W 2-0
Jan 17 1989	Notts County (First Round)	W 2-0
Mar 21 1989	Torquay United (Southern Area Semi-Final)	L 0-1

1989-1990

Barclays League Division Three

Aug 26 1989	Chester City	D 1-1
Sep 9 1989	Bury	L 0-1
Sep 23 1989	Birmingham City	L 0-1
Sep 30 1989	Wigan Athletic	W 3-1
Oct 7 1989	Bristol City	L 0-2
Oct 17 1989	Bolton Wanderers	L 1-2
Oct 28 1989	Fulham	W 2-0
Nov 4 1989	Tranmere Rovers	L 2-4
Dec 3 1989	Leyton Orient	W 4-3
Dec 17 1989	Mansfield Town	W 2-1
Jan 1 1990	Walsall	W 4-0
Jan 6 1990	Rotherham United	W 4-2
Jan 20 1990	Bristol Rovers	W 2-1
Feb 10 1990	Huddersfield Town	W 2-1
Feb 21 1990	Cardiff City	L 0-1
Feb 25 1990	Northampton Town	W 3-2
Mar 10 1990	Crewe Alexandra	L 0-2
Mar 20 1990	Preston North End	D 2-2
Mar 31 1990	Shrewsbury Town	D 1-1
Apr 7 1990	Notts County	L 0-1
Apr 16 1990	Reading	D 1-1
Apr 28 1990	Blackpool	W 5-0
May 2 1990	Swansea City	W 2-1

F.A. Cup

| Nov 18 1989 | Colchester United (First Round) | L 0-1 |

Littlewoods Cup

| Aug 29 1989 | Brighton and Hove Albion (First Round - Second Leg) | D 1-1 |
| Sep 19 1989 | Manchester City (Second Round - First Leg) | W 2-1 |

Leyland DAF Cup

Nov 7 1989	Leyton Orient (Preliminary Round)	W 3-0
Jan 23 1990	Reading (First Round)	W 2-1
Feb 6 1990	Bristol Rovers (Southern Area Quarter-Final)	D 2-2*

Lost 4-3 on penalties.

1990-1991

Barclays League Division Three

Aug 25 1990	AFC Bournemouth	D 0-0
Sep 8 1990	Chester City	L 0-1
Sep 22 1990	Bolton Wanderers	W 4-2
Sep 29 1990	Grimsby Town	W 1-0
Oct 14 1990	Cambridge United	L 0-3
Oct 20 1990	Huddersfield Town	W 1-0
Nov 4 1990	Southend United	L 0-1
Nov 10 1990	Bury	D 2-2
Dec 2 1990	Leyton Orient	W 1-0
Dec 23 1990	Wigan Athletic	W 1-0
Jan 1 1991	Shrewsbury Town	W 3-0
Jan 12 1991	Mansfield Town	D 0-0
Jan 26 1991	Swansea City	W 2-0
Feb 2 1991	Rotherham United	L 1-2
Feb 16 1991	Exeter City	W 1-0
Mar 9 1991	Stoke City	L 0-4
Mar 12 1991	Preston North End	W 2-0
Mar 23 1991	Bradford City	W 6-1
Mar 30 1991	Birmingham City	D 2-2
Apr 6 1991	Crewe Alexandra	W 1-0
Apr 16 1991	Fulham	L 1-2
Apr 27 1991	Reading	W 1-0
May 4 1991	Tranmere Rovers	L 0-2

F.A. Cup

Nov 17 1990	Yeovil Town (First Round)	W 5-0

Rumblelows Cup

Aug 28 1990	Hereford United (First Round - First Leg)	W 2-0
Oct 9 1990	Sheffield Wednesday (Second Round - Second Leg)	L 1-2

Leyland DAF Cup

Jan 29 1991	Leyton Orient (Preliminary Round)	W 2-0
Feb 21 1991	Wrexham (First Round)	D 0-0*
Apr 9 1991	Birmingham City	
	(Southern Area Final - Second Leg)	L 0-1

Won 3-0 on penalties.

Division Three Play Off

May 19 1991	Tranmere Rovers (Semi Final - First Leg)	D 2-2

1991-1992

Barclays League Division Three

Aug 17 1991	Leyton Orient	W 4-3
Aug 31 1991	Huddersfield Town	L 2-3
Sep 14 1991	Reading	W 1-0
Sep 17 1991	Hull City	W 4-1
Sep 28 1991	Bolton Wanderers	W 3-2
Oct 12 1991	Peterborough United	W 2-1
Oct 19 1991	West Bromwich Albion	L 1-2
Nov 6 1991	Birmingham City	D 2-2
Nov 9 1991	Wigan Athletic	W 4-0
Nov 30 1991	Swansea City	W 3-2
Dec 22 1991	Exeter City	W 3-0
Jan 1 1992	Hartlepool United	W 1-0
Jan 11 1992	Stoke City	W 2-0
Jan 25 1992	Preston North End	W 1-0
Feb 8 1992	Bury	L 0-3
Feb 15 1992	Torquay United	W 3-2
Feb 29 1992	Stockport County	W 2-1
Mar 3 1992	Chester City	W 2-0
Mar 14 1992	Bradford City	L 3-4
Mar 29 1992	AFC Bournemouth	D 2-2
Apr 4 1992	Shrewsbury Town	W 2-0
Apr 17 1992	Darlington	W 4-1
Apr 26 1992	Fulham	W 4-0

F.A Cup

Nov 18 1991	Gillingham (First Round)	D 3-3

Rumblelows Cup

Aug 27 1991	Barnet (First Round - Second Leg)	W 3-1
Sep 24 1991	Brighton and Hove Albion	
	(Second Round - First Leg)	W 4-1

Autoglass Trophy

| Dec 17 1991 | Barnet (Preliminary Round) | L 3-6 |

1992-93

Barclays League Division One

Aug 15 1992	Wolverhampton Wanderers	L 0-2
Aug 29 1992	Southend United	W 2-1
Sep 1 1992	Portsmouth	W 4-1
Sep 13 1992	Luton Town	L 1-2
Sep 26 1992	Millwall	D 1-1
Oct 4 1992	Newcastle United	L 1-2
Oct 17 1992	Watford	D 1-1
Oct 31 1992	Bristol City	W 5-1
Nov 7 1992	Charlton Athletic	W 2-0
Nov 21 1992	Grimsby Town	L 1-3
Nov 28 1992	Oxford United	W 1-0
Dec 20 1992	West Ham United	D 0-0
Dec 26 1992	Derby County	W 2-1
Jan 9 1993	Leicester City	L 1-3
Jan 30 1993	Bristol Rovers	L 0-3
Feb 14 1993	Cambridge United	L 0-1
Feb 27 1993	Peterborough United	L 0-1
Mar 9 1993	Tranmere Rovers	L 0-1
Mar 20 1993	Birmingham City	L 0-2
Mar 27 1993	Swindon Town	D 0-0
Apr 6 1993	Sunderland	D 1-1
Apr 12 1993	Notts County	D 2-2
May 1 1993	Barnsley	W 3-1

F.A. Cup

| Jan 2 1993 | Grimsby Town (Third Round) | L 0-2 |

Coca-Cola Cup

| Aug 25 1992 | Fulham (First Round - Second Leg) | W 2-0 |
| Oct 7 1992 | Tottenham Hotspur (Second Round - Second Leg) | L 2-4 |

Anglo-Italian Cup

Sep 29 1992	Oxford United (Preliminary Round)	W 2-0
Nov 24 1992	Lucchese (Group A)	W 1-0
Dec 16 1992	Bari (Group A)	W 2-1
Jan 27 1993	Derby County (Semi-Final - First Leg)	L 3-4

1993-1994

Endsleigh Insurance League Division Two

Aug 14 1993	Exeter City	W 2-1
Aug 28 1993	Reading	W 1-0
Sep 11 1993	Swansea City	D 1-1
Sep 14 1993	Leyton Orient	L 0-1
Sep 25 1993	Port Vale	L 1-2
Oct 16 1993	Wrexham	W 2-1
Oct 30 1993	Barnet	W 1-0
Nov 2 1993	Cardiff City	D 1-1
Nov 20 1993	Burnley	D 0-0
Dec 11 1993	Blackpool	W 3-0
Dec 29 1993	Bradford City	W 2-0
Jan 3 1994	Stockport County	D 1-1
Jan 8 1994	Bristol Rovers	L 3-4
Jan 22 1994	Hartlepool United	W 1-0
Feb 5 1994	York City	D 1-1
Feb 22 1994	Hull City	L 0-3
Feb 26 1994	Rotherham United	D 2-2
Mar 12 1994	Brighton and Hove Albion	D 1-1
Mar 26 1994	Cambridge United	D 3-3
Apr 2 1994	AFC Bournemouth	D 1-1
Apr 9 1994	Fulham	L 1-2
Apr 23 1994	Plymouth Argyle	D 1-1
May 7 1994	Huddersfield Town	L 1-2

F.A. Cup

Dec 4 1993	Cardiff City (Second Round)	L 1-3

Coca-Cola Cup

Aug 17 1993	Watford (First Round - First Leg)	D 2-2

Autoglass Trophy

Nov 9 1993	Wycombe Wanderers (First Round)	L 2-3

1994-1995

Endsleigh Insurance League Division Two

Aug 20 1994	Peterborough United	L 0-1
Aug 30 1994	Rotherham United	W 2-0

Sep 3 1994	Wrexham	L 0-2
Sep 17 1994	Blackpool	W 3-2
Oct 1 1994	Shrewsbury Town	W 1-0
Oct 8 1994	Bristol Rovers	W 3-0
Oct 22 1994	Birmingham City	L 1-2
Nov 5 1994	Hull City	L 0-1
Nov 26 1994	Brighton and Hove Albion	W 2-1
Dec 17 1994	Plymouth Argyle	W 7-0
Dec 26 1994	Leyton Orient	W 3-0
Dec 31 1994	Oxford United	W 2-0
Jan 14 1995	Swansea City	D 0-0
Jan 28 1995	Cambridge United	W 6-0
Feb 11 1995	Bradford City	W 4-3
Feb 21 1995	Huddersfield Town	D 0-0
Mar 4 1995	Crewe Alexandra	W 2-0
Mar 11 1995	Stockport County	W 1-0
Mar 21 1995	Wycombe Wanderers	D 0-0
Apr 1 1995	York City	W 3-0
Apr 15 1995	Chester City	D 1-1
Apr 22 1995	Cardiff City	W 2-0
Apr 29 1995	AFC Bournemouth	L 1-2

F.A. Cup

Nov 22 1994	Cambridge United (First Round replay)	L 1-2

Coca-Cola Cup

Aug 23 1994	Colchester United (First Round - Second Leg)	W 2-0
Sep 27 1994	Tranmere Rovers (Second Round - Second Leg)	D 0-0

Autowindscreens Shield

Nov 8 1994	Gillingham (First Round)	W 3-1
Dec 3 1994	Oxford United (Second Round)	L 1-2

Third Division Play Off

May 17 1995	Huddersfield Town (Semi-Final - Second Leg)	D 1-1*

* Lost 4-3 on penalties.

1995-1996

Endsleigh Insurance League Division Two

Aug 19 1995	Oxford United	W 1-0
Aug 29 1995	Hull City	W 1-0
Sep 2 1995	Swindon Town	L 0-2
Sep 16 1995	Walsall	W 1-0
Sep 30 1995	Chesterfield	L 1-2
Oct 7 1995	Blackpool	L 1-2
Oct 21 1995	Peterborough United	W 3-0
Nov 4 1995	Shrewsbury Town	L 0-2
Nov 25 1995	Bradford City	W 2-1
Dec 9 1995	Bristol Rovers	D 0-0
Dec 26 1995	Brighton and Hove Albion	L 0-1
Jan 20 1996	York City	W 2-0
Jan 30 1996	Wycombe Wanderers	W 1-0
Feb 3 1996	Burnley	W 1-0
Feb 17 1996	Bristol City	D 2-2
Feb 27 1996	Rotherham United	D 1-1
Mar 9 1996	Wrexham	W 1-0
Mar 19 1996	Carlisle United	D 1-1
Mar 23 1996	Swansea City	D 0-0
Apr 2 1996	Stockport County	W 1-0
Apr 6 1996	Crewe Alexandra	W 2-1
Apr 13 1996	Notts County	D 0-0
May 4 1996	AFC Bournemouth	W 2-0

F.A. Cup

Nov 11 1995	Farnborough Town (First Round)	D 1-1

Coca-Cola Cup

Aug 22 1995	Walsall First Round - Second Leg)	W 3-2
Oct 3 1995	Bolton Wanderers (Second Round - Second Leg)	L 2-3

Autowindscreens Shield

Oct 17 1995	Exeter City (First Round)	D 1-1
Nov 28 1995	Fulham (Second Round)	L 0-1

1996-97

Endsleigh Insurance League Division Two

Aug 24 1996	Luton Town	W 3-2
Aug 27 1996	Gillingham	W 2-0
Sep 10 1996	Plymouth Argyle	W 3-2
Sep 14 1996	Blackpool	D 1-1
Sep 28 1996	York City	D 3-3

Oct 5 1996	Rotherham United	W 4-2
Oct 19 1996	Walsall	D 1-1
Oct 26 1996	Millwall	D 0-0
Nov 9 1996	Stockport County	D 2-2
Nov 23 1996	Wrexham	W 2-0
Dec 3 1996	Notts County	W 2-0
Dec 21 1996	Preston North End	D 0-0
Jan 18 1997	Bristol City	D 0-0
Jan 21 1997	Bristol Rovers	D 0-0
Feb 8 1997	Watford	D 1-1
Feb 22 1997	AFC Bournemouth	W 1-0
Mar 4 1997	Wycombe Wanderers	D 0-0
Mar 15 1997	Burnley	L 0-3
Mar 29 1997	Bury	L 0-2
Apr 5 1997	Shrewsbury Town	D 0-0
Apr 15 1997	Chesterfield	W 1-0
Apr 19 1997	Crewe Alexandra	L 0-2
May 3 1997	Peterborough United	L 0-1

F.A. Cup

| Nov 16 1996 | AFC Bournemouth (First Round) | W 2-0 |
| Jan 25 1997 | Manchester City (Third Round) | L 0-1 |

Coca-Cola Cup

| Aug 20 1996 | Plymouth Argyle (First Round - First Leg) | W 1-0 |
| Sep 17 1996 | Blackburn Rovers (Second Round - First Leg) | L 1-2 |

Autowindscreens Shield

| Jan 7 1997 | Barnet (Second Round) | W 2-1 |
| Jan 28 1997 | Colchester United (Southern Area Quarter-Final) | L 0-1 |

Second Division Play Off

| May 14 1997 | Bristol City (Semi Final - Second Leg) | W 2-1 |

1997-98

Endsleigh Insurance League Division Two

Aug 16 1997	Chesterfield	D 0-0
Aug 30 1997	Grimsby Town	W 3-1
Sep 2 1997	Gillingham	W 2-0
Sep 19 1997	Wycombe Wanderers	D 1-1

Sep 27 1997	Burnley	W 2-1
Oct 18 1997	Walsall	W 3-0
Oct 21 1997	Bristol Rovers	L 2-3
Nov 4 1997	Carlisle United	L 0-1
Nov 8 1997	Bristol City	L 1-4
Nov 29 1997	Wrexham	D 1-1
Dec 13 1997	Blackpool	W 3-1
Dec 26 1997	Southend United	D 1-1
Jan 10 1998	Millwall	W 2-1
Jan 24 1998	Watford	L 1-2
Jan 31 1998	Plymouth Argyle	W 3-1
Feb 14 1998	Preston North End	D 0-0
Feb 28 1998	York City	L 1-2
Mar 7 1998	AFC Bournemouth	W 3-2
Mar 21 1998	Northampton Town	D 0-0
Mar 28 1998	Oldham Athletic	W 2-1
Apr 11 1998	Fulham	L 0-2
Apr 18 1998	Wigan Athletic	L 0-2
Apr 25 1998	Luton Town	D 2-2

F.A. Cup

| Nov 15 1997 | Colchester United (First Round) | D 2-2 |

Coca-Cola Cup

| Aug 15 1997 | Shrewsbury Town (First Round - First Leg) | D 1-1 |
| Sep 30 1997 | Southampton (Second Round - Second Leg) | L 0-2 |

1998-1999

Nationwide League Division Three

Aug 8 1998	Mansfield Town	W 3-0
Aug 22 1998	Brighton & Hove Albion	W 2-0
Aug 31 1998	Rochdale	W 2-1
Sep 12 1998	Rotherham United	L 0-3
Sep 26 1998	Darlington	W 3-0
Oct 17 1998	Hartlepool United	W 3-1
Oct 20 1998	Scunthorpe United	W 2-1
Nov 10 1998	Southend United	W 4-1
Nov 28 1998	Chester City	W 2-1
Dec 18 1998	Cambridge United	W 1-0
Dec 28 1998	Cardiff City	W 1-0
Jan 2 1999	Barnet	W 3-1
Feb 2 1999	Carlisle United	D 1-1

Feb 6 1999	Hull City	L 0-2
Feb 13 1999	Torquay United	W 3-2
Feb 27 1999	Scarborough	D 1-1
Mar 9 1999	Peterborough United	W 3-0
Mar 13 1999	Shrewsbury Town	D 0-0
Mar 16 1999	Halifax Town	D 1-1
Apr 5 1999	Plymouth Argyle	W 3-1
Apr 17 1999	Leyton Orient	D 0-0
May 1 1999	Exeter City	W 3-0
May 4 1999	Swansea City	W 4-1

F.A. Cup

| Nov 14 1998 | Camberley Town (First Round) | W 5-0 |
| Dec 15 1998 | Oldham Athletic (Second Round replay) | D 2-2* |

Lost 4-2 on penalties.

Worthington Cup

| Aug 18 1998 | West Bromwich Albion (First Round - Second Leg) | W 3-0 |
| Sep 15 1998 | Tottenham Hotspur (Second Round - First Leg) | L 2-3 |

Autowindscreens Shield

| Dec 8 1998 | Plymouth Argyle (First Round) | W 2-0 |
| Jan 19 1999 | Walsall (Southern Area Quarter-Final) | D 0-0* |

Lost 4-3 on penalties.

1999-2000

Nationwide League Division Two

Aug 14 1999	Oldham Athletic	W 2-0
Aug 28 1999	Blackpool	W 2-0
Sep 18 1999	Luton Town	W 2-0
Sep 25 1999	Preston North End	D 2-2
Sep 28 1999	Cardiff City	W 2-1
Oct 16 1999	Oxford United	W 2-0
Oct 19 1999	Gillingham	L 1-2
Nov 2 1999	Reading	D 1-1
Nov 12 1999	Scunthorpe Unite	W 4-3
Dec 4 1999	Bristol Rovers	L 0-3
Dec 10 1999	Chesterfield	D 1-1
Dec 26 1999	Bristol City	W 2-1
Jan 3 2000	Stoke City	L 0-1
Jan 22 2000	Bury	W 2-1

Feb 5 2000	Notts County	L 0-2
Feb 19 2000	Wycombe Wanderers	D 0-0
Mar 4 2000	Cambridge United	D 1-1
Mar 7 2000	Wrexham	L 0-2
Mar 18 2000	AFC Bournemouth	L 0-2
Apr 1 2000	Wigan Athletic	L 0-2
Apr 15 2000	Millwall	L 1-3
Apr 24 2000	Burnley	L 2-3
May 6 2000	Colchester United	D 0-0

F.A. Cup

| Oct 30 1999 | Plymouth Argyle (First Round) | D 2-2 |

Worthington Cup

| Aug 11 1999 | Ipswich Town (First Round - First Leg) | L 0-2 |

Autowindscreens Shield

| Jan 25 2000 | Oxford United (Southern Area Quarter-Final) | W 2-0 |

2000-2001

Nationwide League Division Two

Aug 19 2000	Swansea City	D 0-0
Aug 28 2000	Bristol Rovers	L 2-6
Sep 2 2000	Wycombe Wanderers	D 0-0
Sep 16 2000	Millwall	D 1-1
Sep 30 2000	AFC Bournemouth	W 3-2
Oct 14 2000	Peterborough United	W 1-0
Oct 17 2000	Colchester United	W 1-0
Oct 28 2000	Walsall	W 2-1
Nov 11 2000	Rotherham United	L 0-3
Dec 2 2000	Wigan Athletic	D 2-2
Dec 23 2000	Oldham Athletic	D 1-1
Jan 1 2001	Oxford United	W 3-0
Jan 6 2001	Northampton Town	D 1-1
Feb 10 2001	Reading	L 1-2
Feb 20 2001	Bristol City	W 2-1
Feb 24 2001	Notts County	W 3-1
Mar 10 2001	Stoke City	D 2-2
Mar 31 2001	Wrexham	W 1-0
Apr 10 2001	Swindon Town	L 0-1
Apr 14 2001	Port Vale	D 1-1
Apr 25 2001	Cambridge United	D 2-2

| May 3 2001 | Luton Town | D 2-2 |
| May 5 2001 | Bury | W 3-1 |

F.A. Cup

| Nov 18 2000 | Kingstonian (First Round) | L 1-3 |

Worthington Cup

| Sep 25 2000 | Bristol City (First Round - Second Leg) | W 2-1 |
| Sep 19 2000 | Tottenham Hotspur (Second Round - First leg) | D 0-0 |

LDV Vans Trophy

Dec 5 2000	Oxford United (First Round)	W 4-1
Jan 9 2001	Brighton and Hove Albion (Second Round)*	D2-2§
Mar 20 2001	Southend United (Southern Area Final)	W 2-1

* Played at Griffin Park due to unfit pitch.
§ Won 4-2 on penalties.

2001-2002

Nationwide League Division Two

Aug 18 2001	Port Vale	W 2-0
Aug 27 2001	Cambridge United	W 2-1
Sep 8 2001	Tranmere Rovers	W 4-0
Sep 18 2001	Bristol City	D 2-2
Sep 22 2001	Oldham Athletic	D 2-2
2Sep 9 2001	Colchester United	W 4-1
Oct 13 2001	Peterborough United	W 2-1
Oct 23 2001	Bury	W 5-1
Nov 3 2001	Blackpool	W 2-0
Nov 24 2001	Queens Park Rangers	D 0-0
Dec 15 2001	Wrexham	W 3-0
Dec 21 2001	Northampton	W 3-0
Jan 19 2002	Wigan Athletic	L 0-1
Jan 24 2002	Brighton and Hove Albion	W 4-0
Feb 9 2002	AFC Bournemouth	W 1-0
Feb 12 2002	Cardiff City	W 2-1
Feb 23 2002	Notts County	W 2-1
Mar 5 2002	Swindon Town	W 2-0
Mar 12 2002	Chesterfield	D 0-0
Mar 16 2002	Wycombe Wanderers	W 1-0
Mar 30 2002	Stoke City	W 1-0

Apr 6 2002	Huddersfield Town	W 3-0
Apr 20 2002	Reading	D 1-1

F.A. Cup

Nov 17 2001	Morecambe	W 1-0

Worthington Cup

Aug 14 2001	Norwich City (First Round)	W1-0

Second Division Play Off

May 1 2002	Huddersfield Town (Semi-Final)	W 2-1

2002-2003

Nationwide League Division Two

Aug 13 2002	Bristol City	W 1-0
Aug 17 2002	Oldham Athletic	D 0-0
Aug 26 2002	Swindon Town	W 3-1
Sep 7 2002	Luton Town	D 0-0
Sep 21 2002	Wycombe Wanderers	W 1-0
Oct 5 2002	Barnsley	L 1-2
Oct 19 2002	Port Vale	D 1-1
Oct 29 2002	Plymouth Argyle	D 0-0
Nov 2 2002	Blackpool	W 5-0
Nov 23 2002	Wigan Athletic	L 0-1
Dec 14 2002	Chesterfield	W 2-1
Dec 28 2002	Mansfield Town	W 1-0
Jan 18 2003	Notts County	D 1-1
Feb 8 2003	Crewe Alexandra	L 1-2
Feb 25 2003	Huddersfield Town	W 1-0
Mar 1 2003	Tranmere Rovers	L 1-2
Mar 4 2003	Cardiff City	L 0-2
Mar 11 2003	Colchester United	D 1-1
Mar 15 2003	Stockport County	L 1-2
Mar 29 2003	Northampton Town	W 3-0
Apr 5 2003	Cheltenham Town	D 2-2
Apr 19 2003	Queens Park Rangers	L 1-2
May 3 2003	Peterborough United	D 1-1

FA. Cup

Jan 4 2003	Derby County (Third Round)	W 1-0
Jan 25 2003	Burnley (Fourth Round)	L 0-3

Worthington Cup

| Oct 1 2002 | Middlesbrough (Second Round) | L 1-4 |

LDV Vans Trophy

| Dec 10 2002 | Kidderminster Harriers (Quarter-Final) | W 2-1 |
| Jan 21 2003 | Cambridge United (Semi-Final) | L 1-2 |

2003-2004

Nationwide League Division Two

Aug 16 2003	Peterborough United	L 0-3
Aug 25 2003	Oldham Athletic	W 2-1
Sep 6 2003	Plymouth Argyle	L 1-3
Sep 16 2003	Blackpool	D 0-0
Sep 20 2003	Hartlepool United	W 2-1
Oct 4 2003	Sheffield Wednesday	L 0-3
Oct 18 2003	Luton Town	W 4-2
Oct 21 2003	Brighton and Hove Albion	W 4-0
Nov 1 2003	Barnsley	W 2-1
Nov 22 2003	Grimsby Town	L 1-3
Dec 20 2003	Swindon Town	L 0-2
Dec 26 2003	Bristol City	L 1-3
Jan 10 2004	Tranmere Rovers	D 2-2
Jan 24 2004	Wrexham	L 0-1
Jan 31 2004	Port Vale	W 3-2
Feb 14 2004	Queens Park Rangers	D 1-1
Feb 28 2004	Notts County	L 2-3
Mar 13 2004	Stockport County	L 0-2
Mar 20 2004	Rushden and Diamonds	W 3-2
Apr 3 2004	Chesterfield	D 1-1
Apr 12 2004	Colchester United	W 3-2
Apr 24 2004	Wycombe Wanderers	D 1-1
May 8 2004	AFC Bournemouth	W 1-0

F.A. Cup

| Nov 8 2003 | Gainsborough Trinity (First Round) | W 7-1 |

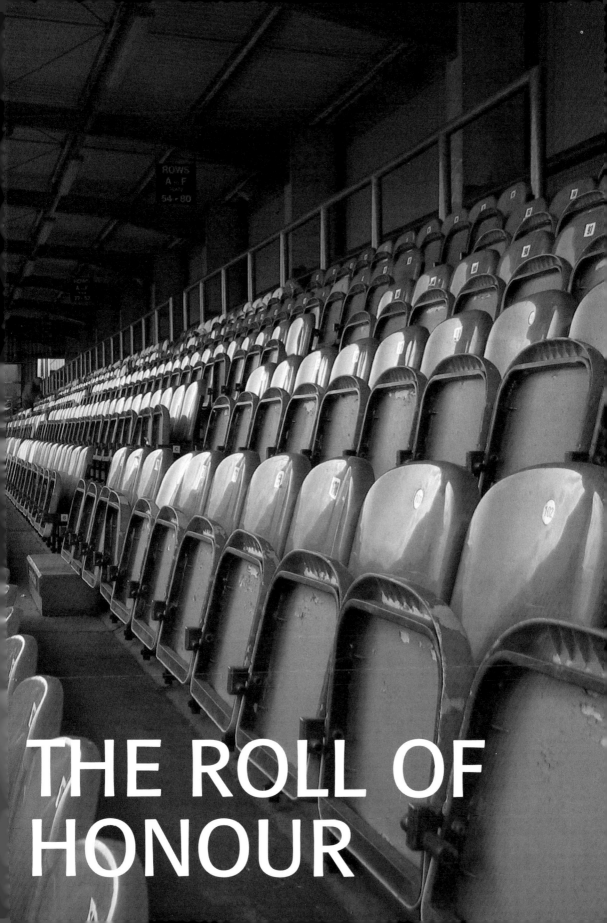

THE ROLL OF HONOUR

THE ROLL OF HONOUR

On behalf of the following, £10 has been donated in order that their names may be recorded in recognition of past or present support of the Club.

1	Jonathan Burchill	Harrow
2	Jamie Burchill	Harrow
3	Peter Richards	Feltham
4	Paul Bryce	Hanwell
5	Emily Bryce	Hanwell
6	Joseph Bryce	Hanwell
7	Steven Cowan	Brentford
8	Caleb Johnstone-Cowan	Brentford
9	Brian Wilson	Sywell
10	Alan Winter	Twickenham
11	Geoffrey Wheeler	Harrow
12	James Wheeler	Harrow
13	Matthew Wheeler	Harrow
14	Barry Mell	Tenterden
15	Stuart Nixon	Greenford
16	Alan Nixon	Cromer
17	Paul Haines	Feltham
18	Colin Haines	Feltham
19	David Cutting	Hampton
20	Ross Cutting	Hampton
21	Paul Martin	Banbury
22	Joseph Martin	Banbury
23	Neil Howard	Hayes
24	Paul Howard	Harlington
25	Helen Carter	Hayes
26	Brian Jay	Northampton
27	Brian Jackson	Hounslow
28	In Memory of Ron Luffrum	Hounslow
29	John Griffin	Staines
30	Margaret Felton	Addlestone
31	Fred Anderson	Isleworth
32	Jack Luckett	Brentford
33	Tim Luckett	Brentford
34	Rose Luckett	Brentford
35	Ginny Luckett	Brentford
36	Martin Barrett	Ealing
37	Robert Barrett	Ealing
38	Adrian Gibson	Worcester Park
39	Paul Gibson	West Molesey
40	Brian Burgess	Wimbledon
41	Rob Staggs	Greenford
42	Catherine Ryan	Hayes End
43	Jason Staggs	Greenford
44	Ray Smith	Langley
45	Stuart Smith	Langley
46	Kevin Fancourt	Dagenham
47	Arthur Claiden	Surbiton
48	Steve Claiden	Chessington
49	Mark Claiden	Chessington
50	Robert Claiden	Richmond-upon-Thames
51	David Claiden	Richmond-upon-Thames
52	Noel Sheldrake	Aylesbury
53	Ron Sheldrake	Aylesbury
54	Glen Sheldrake	Moreton-in-Marsh
55	Thomas Moore	Chiswick
56	Dennis L Moore	Chiswick
57	Andy Zajczyk	South Ealing
58	Alan Maskell	Northampton
59	Ray Evans	Shepperton
60	Shirley Golding	Barnet
61	Stephen Golding	Barnet
62	Cathering Golding	Barnet
63	Paul Spencer (Pauly boy)	Brentford
64	Julie Henry (a real star)	London SW1
65	Jon Gosling	Bishop's Stortford
66	Paul Gosling	Bishop's Stortford
67	Phil Roker	Hammersmith
68	Madalyn Roker	Hammersmith
69	Cameron Roker	Hammersmith
70	Bob Roker	Ickenham
71	Jeremy Clark	Hounslow West
72	Rob Davies	Uxbridge
73	James Davies	Uxbridge
74	Jude Davies	Uxbridge
75	In Memory of Frank Smith	Twickenham
76	Bryan Clark	Ashford
77	Graham Clark	Staines
78	Graham Whitham	Sutton
79	Martin Reed	Stanwell
80	Paul Reed	Stanwell
81	Ian Wright	West Ealing
82	Mark Wright	West Ealing
83	Dick Sangster	West Ealing
84	Larry Signy	Farnham
85	Nick Porter	Ickenham
86	Jasmine Porter	Ickenham
87	Christopher Horricks	Cheshire
88	Mark Czerwonka	Chiswick
89	Alan Matthews	Slough
90	Leighton Matthews	Slough
91	Philip Turner	Hatfield
92	Rod Scales	Camberley
93	Rik Scales	Camberley
94	Phil Silva	Heston
95	David Silva	Heston
96	Jim Priest	Hungerford
97	David Heath	Hillingdon
98	Mark Heath	Hillingdon
99	Colin Quarmby	Hanwell
100	Richard Merritt	Hayes
101	Ryszard Wolski	Isleworth
102	Nikki Wolski	Stockton-on-Tees
103	Graham Rice	Twickenham
104	Lawrence Rice	Twickenham
105	Stuart Hatcher	Greenwich
106	Roy Hatcher	Norfolk
107	Clive Soden	Stonebridge Park
108	David Enstone	Bedfont
109	Richard Thurston	Osney
110	Susanne Higginbottom	Hampshire
111	Mark Pickard	Isleworth
112	Robin Pickard	Isleworth
113	David Cordery	Chertsey
114	Roy Woods	Hounslow
115	Tracy Woods	Hounslow
116	Ian Dawes	Hanwell
117	Roger Beeney	East Grinstead
118	Robert Beeney	London
119	Brian Willman	Richmond-upon-Thames
120	Keith Piggott	Hanwell
121	Gary Piggott	Hanwell
122	Alan Napier	Uxbridge
123	Leonard Grubb (deceased)	Bracknell
124	Patrick Feeley	Houston - U.S.A.
125	Brian Morgan	Ruislip
126	Ken Piggott	Hanwell
127	Paul Szczerbakowicz	Perivale
128	Nick Maniatiakis	Brentford
129	Andy Ditton	Maidenhead
130	John Edwards	Monkton
131	David Edwards	Guildford
132	Barry Bissett	Wootoon Bassett
133	Christine Bissett	Wootoon Bassett
134	Trudy Collett	Paphos - Cyprus
135	Terry Collett	Paphos - Cyprus
136	Laura Collett	Brentford
137	Mark Collett	Brentford
138	Simon Harrison	Harefield
139	Annie Van Damme	Harefield
140	Terence Baynham	Ruislip
141	David Pring	Lichfield
142	Len Wiles	Isleworth
143	Malcolm Smith	Reading
144	Leslie Smith (deceased)	
145	David Furlong	Surbiton
146	Derek Furlong	Walton-on-Thames
147	Kevin Furlong	Surbiton
148	Brian Moriarty	Colnbrook
149	Karon Whitham	Sutton
150	Pete Johnston	Slough
151	Bernie Watson	Virgina Water
152	Peter Smith	Northwood
153	Colin Burkin	Lightwater
154	Ian Burkin	Lightwater
155	Dave Phillips	South Africa
156	Clive Longhurst	Chesham

157	Penny Longhurst	Chesham
158	Bert Longhurst	Amersham
159	Darrin Romp	Waterlooville
160	Howard Lowry	Stourport
161	Joanne Sewell	Heston
162	In memory of Bill Merry	
163	Su Green	Heston
164	Gez Smith	Virgina Water
165	Steve Ramnarain	Chiswick
166	Ad Ramnarain	Chiswick
167	Colin Thurbon	Banbury
168	Jimmy O'Reardon	Luton
169	Jackie Willis	Greenford
170	Tony Willis	Greenford
171	Patrick O'Reardon	Hanwell
172	John O'Reardon	Hanwell
173	Pattrick Hyland	Hanwell
174	James Sugrue	Hayes
175	Bill Darvill	Uxbridge
176	William Darvill	Uxbridge
177	Pauline Darvill	Uxbridge
178	Michael Darvill	Uxbridge
179	Roy King	Brentford
180	Suzanne Darbinson	Whitton
181	Aimee Darbinson	Whitton
182	Leanne Darbinson	Whitton
183	Andrew King	Belverdere
184	Fred King	Erith
185	Fred Larkbey	Whitton
186	Graham Larkbey	Walthamstow
187	Gus Curtis	Hanwell
188	Charles Pabor	Pagnell
189	Graham Sandys	Carshalton
190	Steven Hearne	London
191	David Griffith	Dudley
192	Jill Griffith	Erdington
193	Luke Kirton	Brentford
194	Mary Kirton	Brentford
195	Lisa Tomkins	Hounslow
196	Danny Tomkins	Honuslow
197	Summer Tomkins	Hounslow
198	Peter Barnard	Dunsfold
199	Allison Barnard	Dunsfold
200	Denis Barnard (deceased)	
201	Danielle Wayne	Swindon
202	Caroline Chamberlain	Heston
203	Georgina Newton	Heston
204	Chris Chamberlain	Heston
205	Robert Chamberlain	Heston
206	Pat Chamberlain	Heston
207	Roger Fuller	Chelmsford
208	Mark Fuller	Chelmsford
209	Paul Fuller	Braintree
210	Alan Schollar	Worthing
211	Sidney Hockley	Ealing
212	Elaine Schollar	Mitcham
213	Steve Schollar	Newbury
214	Kenneth Crabb	Buckinghamshire
215	Ian Skull	Feltham
216	Marie Skull	Hanwell
217	Amy Howard	Ealing
218	David Stallabrass	Chalfont St Peter
219	James Slade	Reading
220	Linda Slade	Reading
221	Robert Walker	Milton Keynes
222	Tony Davis	Hanwell
223	Gary Davis	Twickenham
224	Derek Peters	Staines
225	Tonia Stimpson	Uxbridge
226	Paul Hayward -Lynch	Uxbridge
227	Clive Brooks	Brentford
228	Owen Brooks	Brentford
229	Leslie Brooks	Brentford
230	Emma Brooks	Brentford
231	In memory of David Westbrook	Staines
232	Ian Westbrook	London
233	Hugh Westbrook	London
234	Peter McDonald	Iver Heath
235	Kate Cousins	Clacton
236	Andy Griffin	Teddington
237	Don Griffin	Hampton
238	Simon Griffin	Hampton Hill
239	Margaret Weston (nee Grums)	Twickenham
240	Matt Wilkins	Belsize Park
241	John Barr	Staines
242	Brian Barr	Staines
243	Cliff Barr	Florida - U.S.A
244	In memory of Dennis Barr	Cape Town
245	John P Barr	Teddington
246	Mark Rand	Ealing
247	Matthew Rand	Ealing
248	In memory of Clinton Mitchell	Brentwood
249	Alan Scott	Sunbury
250	Brian Egan	Maidenhead
251	Mark Egan	Maidenhead
252	Henry Egan	Maidenhead
253	Charlie Egan	Maidenhead
254	Keith Harris	North Hykeham
255	Eric Harris	North Hykeham
256	John O'Keeffe	Swindon
257	Robin Pearson	Isleworth
258	Rachel Pearson	Ashtead
259	In memory of Derek Pearson	Richmond-upon-Thames
260	Richard Marson	Hayes
261	In memory of George Marson	Hayes
262	In memory of Philip Barney	Hayes
263	Emily Briggs	Isleworth
264	John Pitt	Heston
265	Matthew Pitt	Heston
266	Dr Sarah Pitt	Heston
267	Luke Hulatt	Ashford
268	Katherine Hulatt	Ashford
269	Ken Hart	Pinner
270	Georgina Thompson	Chiswick
271	Paul Thompson	Chiswick
272	Michael Carter	St. Neots
273	Gary Murphy	Isleworth
274	Lyndsey Moore	Isleworth
275	Doug Collins	Isleworth
276	Stuart Cleveland	Hounslow
277	Sian Giddens	Hounslow
278	Brian Clark	Bedfont
279	Jason Clark	Hanworth
280	Christine Clark	Hanworth
281	Alan Clark	Hanworth
282	Derek Hazel	Ashford
283	Harry Dando	Beckley
284	Michael Wareham	Canada
285	Chris Beesley	Wokingham
286	Robert Wood	Holyport
287	Brian Field	London
288	In loving memory of Thomas Field	Hounslow
289	David Tibble	Sunbury
290	Douglas Tibble	Hailsham
291	Edward Henning (deceased)	Chiswick
292	Ted Henning	Surbiton
293	Alex Henning	Bournemouth
294	Andrew Henning	Poole
295	Thomas Henning	Poole
296	Michael Cabble	Isleworth
297	John Edwards	Lane End
298	Gary Lahr	Deal
299	Jack Lahr	Deal
300	Stephen Goringe	Twickenham
301	Marcus Goringe	Twickenham
302	In memory of Frank Dean	Hampton
303	Peter Dean	Dover
304	Malcolm Hobday	Isleworth
305	Neil Knightley	Isleworth
306	John Evans Snr (deceased)	South Ealing
307	Gary Edge	Chiswick
308	Philip Edge	Chiswick
309	Robert Griffiths	Thame
310	Barry Neighbour	Little Sandhurst
311	Lee Ashton	Brighton
312	Keith Middleton	Bedfont
313	John Stride	East Sheen
314	Matthew Stride	East Sheen
315	Helen Stride	East Sheen
316	Jim Walsh	Hayes
317	William Walsh	Hayes
318	Phil Walsh	Hayes
319	John Barry	Hayes
320	Nikki Evans	Egham

321	John Evans	Egham
322	Sam Evans	Egham
323	Lucy Caller	Shepperton
324	Malcolm Graham	Charing
325	Shirley Tassell	Charing
326	Neil Plunkett	Ashford
327	Les Plunkett	Ashford
328	Herbert Lewry	Hanwell
329	Clive Lewry	Whitton
330	Peter Lewry	Whitton
331	Gemma Lewry	Whitton
332	John McGlashan	Ashford
333	Mary McGlashan	Ashford
334	Andrew McGlashan	Ashford
335	Steven McGlashan	Ashford
336	Malcolm Capon	Hanworth
337	David Murphy	Hampton
338	Gemma Murphy	Hampton
339	David Lyons	Camelford
340	Brian Flanagan	Uxbridge
341	David Carter	Brentford
342	Clive Carter	West Drayton
343	Clive Baker	Eastcote
344	David Thurbon	Aylesbury
345	Chris How	Belgium
346	Andy Dean	Bracknell
347	Warren Dean	Bracknell
348	Cliff Dean	Hillingdon
349	Anthony Cornish	Ashford (Middlesex)
350	William Cornish	Sunbury
351	Peter Stevens	Isleworth
352	Stanley Willis	Richmond-upon-Thames
353	The Besants	Feltham
354	Keith Langton	Wokingham
355	Lyn Langton	Wokingham
356	Ronald Langton	Wokingham
357	John Meade	Harlington
358	Melvin Collins	Brentford
359	Bruce Powell	Ickenham
360	Christine Powell	Ickenham
361	Jon Powell	Lingfield
362	Tim Powell	Lingfield
363	Joyce Neate	Chiswick
364	In loving memory of Bill Neate	Chiswick
365	In loving memory of Bill Cooper	Chiswick
366	In loving memory of Ivy Cooper	Chiswick
367	Garrie Bridle	Chessington
368	Robert Bridle	Chessington
369	Bob Bridle	Acton
370	Jefferey Bridle	Chiswick
371	Christopher Bridle	Chiswick
372	Richard Bridle	Northolt
373	Paul Bridle	Bedford
374	Lynne Morgan	Shepperton
375	Ben Wildman	Shepperton
376	Seppo Kuusinen	London
377	John Warren	Chiswick
378	Keith Warren	Hitchin
379	Geoffrey John Chandler	Ealing
380	Dennis Fruin	Feltham
381	Graham Fruin	Feltham
382	Bill Axbey	Ealing
383	Andrew Chapman	Acton Green
384	Colin Downey	Hounslow
385	Matthew Downey	Hounslow
386	James Frederick Collins	Chiswick
387	Greg Heath	Lambourn
388	Mel Paisley	Bristol
389	Richard Heath	Reading
390	Caroline Heath	Reading
391	Geoff Vial	Bedfont
392	Des Fielder	Heston
393	Jonathan Woodard	Brentford
394	David Woodard	Ealing
395	John McEnery	Hounslow
396	Gordon Manning	Isleworth
397	Sandra Jordan	Blyth
398	Andrew Stirling	Chiswick
399	Philip Dear	Hounslow
400	Martin Goold	Hayes
401	Steven Goold	Hayes
402	Jamie Goold	Hayes
403	Not Well Army	Griffin Park
404	David Ohl	Richmond-upon-Thames
405	Mark Walter	Chessington
406	Stephen Walter	Chessington
407	Peter Walter	Chessington
408	Alan Walter	Chessington
409	Daniel Walter	Chessington
410	Paul Langford	Woking
411	Kevin Bere	Bondi Beach
412	Paul Merritt	Leicester
413	Tony Slade	Wallington
414	Darrell Goddard	Brentford
415	Oliver Goodard	Brentford
416	Ian Humphries	Hounslow
417	Vic Humphries	Hounslow
418	Harry Humphries	Osterley
419	Stephen Humpries	Ashford
420	Janet Humphries	Ashford
421	John Huggins	Hounslow
422	Alan Fowler	Ealing
423	Trevor Dearden	Ealing
424	Colin Bevis	Frimley
425	Brian Bevis (deceased)	Staines
426	Jan Wells	West Sussex
427	Reg Wells	West Sussex
428	Peter Gilham	Hampton Hill
429	Adrienne Gilham	Hampton Hill
430	Ron Gilham	Ruislip
431	Dominic Gilham	West Drayton
432	Martin Allen	Brentford FC
433	Adrian Whitbread	Brentford FC
434	Denis Spencer	Ealing
435	Ian Venner	Hayes
436	Richard Leahy Senior	Hanwell
437	Richard Leahy Junior	Dorking
438	Stephen Callen	Richmond-upon-Thames
439	In memory of Hugh McHugh	Chiswick
440	Kieran Feltham	Hillingdon
441	Robert Spenceley	Milton Keynes
442	Paul Duval	Hazelmere
443	Michael Duval	Hazelmere
444	Samantha Duval	Hazelmere
445	Brian Arnold	Thames Ditton
446	Adrian Arnold	Surbition
447	Harry Arnold	Surbition
448	Roy Daniels	Pershore
449	David Daniels	Marchington
450	Andy Sneddon	Feltham
451	The Rowland Family	Ruislip
452	Pete Crook	Brentford
453	Steve Flanagan	West Ealing
454	Lee Brooks	West Ealing
455	Megan Pike	Egham
456	Steve Pike	Egham
457	Norman Pike	Egham
458	Alan Gilding	Hounslow
459	Ian Gilding	Hounslow
460	Katie Pearce	Twickenham
461	David Tutill	Wokingham
462	Robert Sarfaty	Kingston
463	Damien Sarfaty	Kingston
464	Adam Sarfaty	Kingston
465	Marc Langham	Kingston
466	Gerard McCormack	Harrow
467	Richard Nabarro	Isleworth
468	Brian Wilkins	East Sussex
469	Matt Wilkins	Whitby
470	Andy Saw	Hillingdon
471	Ben Glover	Southall
472	Jamie Channell-Saw	Southall
473	Leonie Channell	Southall
474	Karen Channell	Southall
475	Burt Saw	Hillingdon
476	Becky Wickham	Ealing
477	Chris Wickham	Ealing
478	Michael Wickham	Ealing
479	Peter Wickham	Ealing
480	Gary Scammell	Hanwell
481	David Scammell	Hanwell
482	Phyl Bailey	Hounslow
483	Peter Bailey	Hounslow
484	Ray Bailey	Hounslow

485	Sam Bailey	Hounslow
486	Hannah Bailey	Hounslow
487	Tony Bailey	Hounslow
488	The Late George Bailey	Hounslow
489	Jack Mayes	Hounslow
490	Joe Moran	Greenford
491	Nick Rints	Flackwell Heath
492	Dave Holman	Cobham
493	In memory of W. S. (Bill) Holman	Cobham
494	Bill Pyle	Watford
495	David Pyle	Hemel Hempstead
496	Peter Pyle	North Capel
497	Barrie Pyle	Shrewsbury
498	Kevin Smith	Sunbury
499	Andrew Smith	Sunbury
500	Robert Lampert	Wembley
501	Nik Jacques	Chertsey
502	Sam Jacques	Chertsey
503	Steve Brown	Bracknell
504	Dennis Brown	Bracknell
505	Robert Seijas	Essex
506	Geoff Wheeler	Harrow
507	David Ettridge	Peterborough
508	In memory of Bill Ettridge	Peterborough
509	Frederick Wayne (deceased)	Chertsey
510	Ernie Green	Hounslow
511	Ross Smitheman	Twickenham
512	Stephen Davies	Brentford
513	Jane Davies	Brentford
514	Simon Webster	Croydon
515	Alfred Jenkins	Saskatchewan - Canada
516	Malcolm Jenkins	Saskatchewan - Canada
517	Matthew Jenkins	Alberta - Canada
518	Tiago Jenkins	Alberta - Canada
519	Kim Harding	Hampton
520	Alice Chambers-Harding	Hampton
521	Robert Stevens	Ashford (Middlesex)
522	William Stevens	Stourport on Severn
523	In memory of Elaine Stevens	Stourport on Severn
524	In memory of John Hawkins	Feltham
525	Keith Sturgess	Hanworth
526	Joy Sturgess	Hanworth
527	Robert Osborne	Aylesbury
528	Dennis Osborne	Marlow
529	Martin Osborne	Maidenhead
530	Gerald Osborne	Whitton
531	James Farnden	Brentford
532	Ray Farnden	Isleworth
533	Peter Ginger	Bedfont
534	Mark Ginger	Bedfont
535	Martin Chambers	West Drayton
536	No Coat	Twickenham
537	In memory of Awyn Powell	Ickenham
538	Mary Farley	Hanwell
539	In memory of Albert Farley	Hanwell
540	In memory of Annie Farley	Hanwell
541	In memory of Edward Farley	Hanwell
542	Frank Burgess	Harlington
543	Katie Burgess	Loughborough
544	Jeff Kennedy	Ascot
545	Liam Kennedy	Ascot
546	Peter Hamblen	Crowthorne
547	Richard Hamblen	Swadlincote
548	In memory of Les Willis	Richmond-upon-Thames
549	Philip Clarke	Twickenham
550	Reg Rush (deceased)	Winchester
551	Kelvin Rush	Winchester
552	Steven Rush	Brighton
553	David Rush	Brighton
554	Ian Webb	Ashford
555	John Webb	Sunbury
556	Brenda Webb	Sunbury
557	Johnathon Webb	Sunbury
558	Karen Richardson	Egham
559	Steve Richardson	Egham
560	Charlie Richardson	Egham
561	Molly Richardson	Egham
562	Glen Fallowfield	Otago New Zealand
563	David McKiernan	Ealing
564	Gillian Satchell	Ealing
565	John Garrigan	Rugby
566	Robert Whale	Twyford
567	James Whale	Twyford
568	Paul Bussetti	Ealing
569	Cathy Bussetti	Ealing
570	Stephen Bussetti	Ealing
571	Christopher Bussetti	Ealing
572	John Lovesey	Ewell
573	Colin Lovesey	Sydney - Australia
574	Richard Lovesey	Epsom Downs
575	Robert Lovesey	Ewell
576	In memory of Fred Hale	Southall
577	Brian Potter	Northfields
578	Robert Muttitt	Hayes
579	John Ashton	Eastbourne
580	David Ashton	Eastbourne
581	John Hirdle	Hounslow
582	Barry Keene	Hertford
583	Chas Callaghan	Brentford
584	Joanna Risbey	Farnborough
585	Roy Studds	Ealing
586	Tracey Studds	Feltham
587	Stephen Lenton	Orpington
588	James Lenton	Orpington
589	Frank Barry	Ealing
590	In memory of Patrick Barry	Ealing
591	Clifford Knowles	Crawley
592	Johnathon Ilett	Haultwick
593	Peter Ilett	Ickenham
594	David Ilett	Haultwick
595	Paul Vernon	Wantage
596	George Vernon	Wantage
597	Jack Williams	Garelochhead
598	Robin Williams	Camberley
599	Peter Williams	Farnborough
600	Tony Murphy	Upper Hutt
601	Bill Cork	Hanwell
602	Keith Punnett	Crawley
603	Jason Punnett	Crawley
604	Daniel Punnett	Crawley
605	June Howard	Crawley
606	Ray Howard	Crawley
607	In memory of Sidney Punnett	Crawley
608	Mark Chapman	Twickenham
609	Arran Matthews	Tylers Green
610	In memory of Tom Twydell	Hazlemere
611	Len Edney	
612	Richard Sandall	Isleworth
613	Matt Dolman	London
614	Phil Cook	Pinner
615	Reg Cook	Eastcote
616	Peter Atkinson	Sutton
617	Ken Atkinson	Twickenham
618	Terry Good	Watford
619	Emma Good	Watford
620	Kate Good	Watford
621	Eric Miller	Ruislip
622	Peter Miller (deceased)	
623	Keith Warren	Ealing
624	Michael Cummins	Ruislip
625	Chris Hayward	Ryde
626	Brian Ritchie	Toddington
627	Thomas Ritchie	Toddington
628	Lee Simmonds	Little Chalfont
629	David Simmonds	Little Chalfont
630	Michael Simmonds	Little Chalfont
631	David Langrish	Feltham
632	Douglas Langrish (RIP)	
633	Malcolm Porter	Flackwell Heath
634	Tracy Porter	Flackwell Heath
635	Nicola Porter	Flackwell Heath
636	Dean Porter	Flackwell Heath
637	Patrick O'Neill	Barnes
638	Jill Dawson	Northolt
639	Steven Hedges	Crawley
640	Eamonn Sylvester	Brentford
641	Gary Pain	Farnborough
642	Paul Honhold	Chiswick
643	In memory of Vic Honhold	
644	Brian R Watson	Northolt
645	Brian F Watson	Northolt
646	Simon Allford	Tunbridge Wells
647	George William Cox	Isleworth
648	John Henry Cox	Ashford

649	Derek White	Aston Clinton Bucks
650	Nicholas White	Aston Clinton Bucks
651	In memory of Marjorie 'Lonnie' Lonnen	
652	John Lonnen	Isleworth
653	In memory of Marjorie Lonnen	
654	Caroline Collins (nee Lonnen)	Newbury
655	Debbie Lonnen	Bristol
656	In memory of Dick Harrison	
657	David Harrison	
658	Terry Covacie	Heston
659	Jacky Covacie	Heston
660	Peter King	Petersham
661	Timonthy King	Petersham
662	James King	Petersham
663	David Nott	Hurstpierpoint
664	Frances Martin	Heston
665	Brian Martin	Heston
666	Colin Martin	Hampshire
667	Alba Siletti	Ealing
668	Stephen Hardwick	
669	Paul Murphy	Hampton
670	Della Murphy	Hampton
671	Peter Hewstone	Twickenham
672	Ron Maskell	Reading
673	Gerard Daly	Hanwell
674	James Englefield	
675	Ben Englefield	
676	Russell Wallman	West Dulwich
677	Jo Wallman	West Dulwich
678	Kristina Wallman	West Dulwich
679	Ishka Wallman	West Dulwich
680	John Humphries	Essex
381	Iain Rowsell	Shepperton
682	Ken Rowsell	Shepperton
683	In memory of Eric Bassham	Brentford
684	Chris Swatton	Waddesdon
685	Rebecca Swatton	Waddesdon
686	Tim Wheatley	Farnham
687	Toby Wheatley	Aylesbury
688	Matt Wheatley	Lodsworth
689	Ben Heavens	Northolt
690	Jordan Durban	Northolt
691	Robert Tebby	Aylesbury
692	Ralph Tebby	Aylesbury
693	The late Frank Nicholson	Northolt
694	Ron Cooper	High Wycombe
695	Andrew Cooper	Hong Kong
696	William Bull	Ham
697	Edward Attwood	Sutton
698	Primrose Bull	Ham
699	Reubon Bull	Ham
700	Alan Galley	Brentford
701	Ray Harrison	Hanwell
702	Lesley E Harrison	Hanwell
703	David R Harrison	Hanwell
704	Paul Harrison	Isleworth
705	Suzanne L Harrison	Hanwell
706	John Carroll	Acton
707	Laura Carroll	Acton
708	Daniel Carroll	Acton
709	Nicola Carroll	Acton
710	Carol Carroll	Acton
711	Sheila Carroll	Acton
712	In memory of Bill Carroll	Acton
713	In memory of Ted Carroll	Acton
714	In memory of Dorothy Carroll	Acton
715	In memory of Roy Nash	Hanwell
716	In memory of Ron Allen	Hanwell
717	Roy Tucker	South Ealing
718	Roy Woolsey	Stanmore
719	Mick Cox	Letchworth
720	Nicole Cox	Letchworth
721	Sophie Cox	Letchworth
722	Max Brentford Cox	Letchworth
723	Nicola Cox	Letchworth
724	Alex Watson	Loughton
725	Ray Silver	Didcot
726	Alan Wheatley	Brentford
727	Ray Edwards	Harrow
728	Harvey Edwards	Harrow
729	Pat Prescott	Harrow
730	James Carmichael	Hemel Hempstead
731	Timothy Carmichael	Hemel Hempstead
732	Pip Egan	Brentford
733	Kenneth Bowden	Wokingham
734	Sean Cudmore	London
735	Liam Cudmore	London
736	John Cudmore	London
737	Deborah Horwood	Putney
738	Peter Horwood	Brentford
739	David Hawes	Egham
740	Connor Hawes	Egham
741	Michael Hawes	Egham
742	Michael Hawes (deceased)	Egham
743	Jean Hawes (deceased)	Egham
744	Steve Pyle	Pinner
745	Mike Scantlin	Whitton
746	Robert Winstanley	Scotland
747	Rose Winstanley	Scotland
748	Daniel Powell	Sunbury
749	Jamie Powell	Sunbury
750	Denis Hawkins	Hanwell
751	Malcolm Bere	South Harrow
752	Frank Hunt	Edgware
753	The Goodhall Family	Bracknell
754	George Smith (1930 - 2004)	Isleworth
755	Gary Smith	Isleworth
756	Simon Ambrose	Hillingdon
757	Chris Ambrose	Heston
758	Jake Ambrose	Hillingdon
759	Finley Ambrose	Hillingdon
760	In Memory of Keith Ambrose	
761	Tim Ambrose	Ashford
762	Kate Robinson	Westbourne Park
763	Gary Paul	Hounslow
764	Edward Soudan	Scrapton Farm
765	Thomas Soudan	East Acton
767	Daniel E Mann	Osterley
768	Basil H Mann	Osterley
769	John Sear	Wimbledon
770	George Sear (deceased)	Wimbledon
771	Victor Hurd	Alton
772	Peter Card	Staines
773	Michael Scoates	Crawley
774	Martin Strange	Fleet
775	John Coyle	Southall
776	Chris Whittart	Feltham
777	Scott Whittart	Feltham
778	Edward George Baldwin	Norfolk
779	Phil Baldwin	Gloucestershire
780	Helena Robinson	Esher
781	Ian Robinson	Esher
782	Richard Robinson	Esher
783	Bill Billings	Maidenhead
784	Michael Williams	Hanworth
785	Angelina Williams	Hanworth
786	Tyler Williams	Hanworth
787	Barrell Family	Rochester
788	In memory of John Houghton	Ealing
789	Madeleine Tarrant	Feltham
790	Kevin Chippendale	Leeds
791	Neil Chippendale	NSW - Australia
792	Russell Barker	Acton
793	Joyce Barker	Acton
794	Michael Reynolds	Acton
795	Keith Lee	Chessington
796	Derek Lester	Ealing
797	Mark Taylor	Coventry
798	Brentford Supporters Blind Association	
799	Alan Rogers	Windsor
800	J Snelling (deceased)	Acton Green
801	G F Snelling (deceased)	Acton Green
803	G A Hunt	Acton Green
804	Keith MacInnes	East Grinstead
805	Jan MacInnes	East Grinstead
806	Liam Mordue	East Grinstead
807	Jordan Mordue	East Grinstead
808	Bryan Searle	Hampton
809	Mark Burridge	Ascot
810	Sarah Brough	Ascot
811	Derek Burridge	Notting Hill
812	Jason Travers	Ruislip
813	Barry Lister	Northolt
814	Maureen Lister	Northolt

815	Daniel Lister	Northolt
816	Matthew Lister	Northolt
817	Louise Staines	Feltham
818	Keith Riley	Southampton
819	Ian Anderson	Isleworth
820	Elliot Shaw	Whitton
821	Alasdair Shaw	Whitton
822	Gerry Shaw	Whitton
823	Nigel Shaw	Abingdon
824	Reg Dennett	
825	Phil Moroney	
826	Alan Stenning	Stanwell Moor
827	Carole Stenning	Stanwell Moor
828	Reece Smither	Sunbury
829	Nigel English	Wrasbury
830	Justin Bremner	Brentford
831	Toby Vander Meersch	Brentford
832	Jim Vander Meersch	Billericay
833	Jack Vander Meersch	Billericay
834	Peter Jeffery	Stanwell
835	Mary Jeffery	Stanwell
836	Paul Jeffery	Shepperton
837	Kayden Jeffery	Shepperton
838	Andy Mutton	Hitchin

CORPORATE ROLL OF HONOUR

Aptus Consultants
People Dynamics
R K W Foods
Cambridge Electronics Europe Ltd
Sutton Barnard LTD
Neil Williams Associates Ltd
Geoff Buckingham & Co
Tapsell & Graham Ltd
David A Lyons Associates
Spark Promotions Ltd
Capital Estate Agency
www.beezkneez.org.uk
Gordon Manning Ltd
Robert Neil Hairdressing
ECS
The Brentford Lifeline Society
Avventura
Petrochemicals Logistics Ltd
BIAS
The ABeeC Party